Voices *Of*
Reason

Praise For *Voices Of Reason*

"Moral character is often the missing ingredient in business. In *Voices of Reason*, Robert Begley shows how to turn that trait into a competitive advantage. After years in the C-suite space, I can attest that this essential quality is rare. This book is a powerful guide for reclaiming ethos strategically in business."

—Buffi Gresh, VP of Sales Operations and Author

"In the courtroom, persuasion is key. Robert Begley masterfully applies the timeless principles of *ethos, logos,* and *pathos* to modern leadership and advocacy. As a prosecutor, I relied on these elements—credibility, logic, and emotional resonance—to persuade juries beyond a reasonable doubt. *Voices of Reason* is an indispensable guide for professionals who want to sharpen their persuasive edge and make their message unforgettable."

—James S. Valliant, Retired District Attorney and Author

"Robert Begley gives voice to a truth we see every day at LIBRE—immigrants who come to America in search of freedom often have the most powerful stories, but not always the tools to tell them. *Voices of Reason* changes that. It's a vital guide for anyone who wants to speak with clarity, courage, and conviction about the American Dream."

—Jeffrey Baldwin, Director, The LIBRE Institute

"Robert Begley is not just a masterful speaking coach; he's a man of deep integrity. Your voice matters and he will show you how to make it unforgettable. *Voices of Reason* ignites a battle cry for those who believe in the power of words to shape history, stir souls, and defend liberty. If you want to command a room, move minds, and leave a lasting legacy, read this book."

—Leopold Ajami, Ethical Persuasion & Public Speaking Coach,
Founder of Novel Philosophy Academy

"Robert Begley guides readers of *Voices of Reason* through a panoramic sweep of philosophy, history, and oratory—from Aristotle's timeless insights to the soaring eloquence of Martin Luther King, Jr. His aim? To help you become a more effective speaker—deeply connected to your subject, fully invested in your words, and attuned to your audience. Blending the Logos-Ethos-Pathos framework with detailed analysis of extraordinary speeches, Begley provides tools to elevate your voice in any arena and propel you forward."

—Daniel Modell, Lieutenant (ret.), NYPD, Author, and Entrepreneur

"This book doesn't just celebrate great speeches, such as those by Abraham Lincoln, Frederick Douglass, and Martin Luther King, Jr.; it breaks them down and rebuilds them into a framework you can apply. Whether you're a seasoned speaker or just finding your voice, *Voices of Reason* is your guide to speaking with courage, clarity, and conviction. In a world where too many are silent when it matters most, this book equips you to stand up, speak out, and leave a lasting impact. This book will be the gift that keeps on giving to you and your audiences."

—Craig Valentine, World Champion Speaker, Author, Coach

"Pro-liberty thought leaders and activists today are eager to speak out, be heard, and gain followers, but few know how to do so intelligently, persuasively, or sustainably. Begley offers valuable means for closing the gap. His book presents actionable principles for effective public argumentation, building creatively on Aristotle's 'three pillars of persuasion.' Many can inform, inspire, or instigate separately, but Begley shows how to combine the three for maximum impact. This is a wise and workable guide to the power of persuasion for those who know already the power of ideas."

—Richard M. Salsman, President of InterMarket Forecasting, Inc. and Professor of Political Economy, Duke University

"In a time when powerful voices shape our world, Robert Begley's *Voices of Reason* equips you with the tools to become one of them. This compelling guide analyzes what made history's greatest advocates for liberty so persuasive while offering practical strategies to overcome your speaking fears. You'll discover how mastering communication transforms ordinary individuals into extraordinary leaders—whether at a podium, in a boardroom, or around a dinner table. Robert's principles will empower you to speak with such clarity and conviction that others cannot help but listen. For anyone yearning to make a meaningful impact in the fight for freedom, this indispensable book illuminates the path from silence to significance."

—Daniel Richards, CEO & Chief Rhetorician, Return on Ideas

Voices *Of* Reason

Lessons For Liberty's Leaders

Robert Begley

INDIE BOOKS
INTERNATIONAL

Voices *Of* Reason
Lessons For Liberty's Leaders

© 2025 by Robert Begley

ISBN 13: 978-1-966168-36-2
Library of Congress Control Number: 2025915432

Designed by Melissa Farr, Back Porch Creative, LLC

INDIE BOOKS INTERNATIONAL®, INC.
2511 WOODLANDS WAY
OCEANSIDE, CA 92054
www.indiebooksintl.com

To Carrie-Ann Biondi
(and, also, to those who risk their lives
by lifting their voices to promote liberty)

Table Of Contents

Foreword

by Ford Saeks, CEO, Prime Concepts Group, Inc.

I n today's rapidly evolving digital landscape, where artificial intelligence (AI) is reshaping industries, the timeless principles of effective communication remain paramount. Robert Begley's *Voices of Reason: Lessons for Liberty's Leaders* delves into Aristotle's foundational concepts of ethos, logos, and pathos, illustrating their enduring relevance through the lives and speeches of seven influential figures: Patrick Henry, Abraham Lincoln, Frederick Douglass, Winston Churchill, Martin Luther King, Jr., Ayn Rand, and Magatte Wade.

Ethos: Establishing Trust In The Digital Age

Ethos, representing credibility and moral character, is essential in both human interactions and technological applications. Leaders like Patrick Henry and Frederick Douglass exemplified this through their unwavering commitment to their principles. In the realm of AI, establishing trust is crucial. Just as these leaders built their ethos through consistent actions and integrity, AI systems must be transparent and reliable to gain user confidence.

Logos: The Power Of Logical Appeal

Logos, the appeal to reason and logic, is a cornerstone of persuasive communication. Abraham Lincoln's structured arguments and Ayn Rand's philosophical discourses showcase the effectiveness of logical reasoning. In AI, algorithms and data-driven decisions must be presented clearly to ensure users understand and trust the outcomes.

Pathos: Connecting Emotionally In A Technological World

Pathos, the emotional appeal, is vital for forging connections. Martin Luther King, Jr.'s speeches moved hearts and minds, demonstrating the power of emotional resonance. While AI can analyze and respond to human emotions to some extent, the genuine emotional connections that leaders like MLK fostered remain uniquely human.

Voices of Reason bridges the gap between historical rhetorical mastery and contemporary challenges. By studying these leaders, readers gain insights into effective communication strategies that transcend time. In an era dominated by technology, integrating these timeless principles ensures that our messages remain impactful and authentic.

Robert Begley's work serves as a reminder that while tools and platforms evolve, the core tenets of persuasive communication endure. For anyone seeking to lead, inspire, and connect in today's world, embracing the lessons from *Voices of Reason* is not just beneficial—it's essential.

PART I

Setting
The Stage

CHAPTER 1

The Joy Of Speaking And Why It Matters

"One of my greatest joys in life is speaking; can you identify with that?"
—LES BROWN[1]

Motivational Speakers Hall of Famer Les Brown asks a simple but powerful question about the joy of speaking. If you've experienced the thrill of expressing yourself with clarity and confidence, of seeing people's eyes light up as they grasp your message, you know exactly what he means. Speaking isn't just about transferring information; it's also about connecting, inspiring, and leading.

Yet, for many, the idea of public speaking is anything but joyful. Fear holds them back. Doubt keeps them silent. But what if I told you that speaking could become one of the most empowering skills you'll ever develop?

Who are your heroes of the spoken word? Perhaps you admire the eloquence, charisma, and optimism of John F. Kennedy or the commanding presence and unwavering confidence of Margaret Thatcher. Maybe you enjoy revolutionary product presentations that use storytelling, such as those delivered by Steve Jobs. You could be drawn to the moral conviction, humility, and power of reconciliation of Nelson Mandela. What about the high energy, psychology, and storytelling of Tony Robbins? More recently, there are Brené Brown's moving talks on vulnerability, leadership, and courage. We typically only see these speakers' results: riveting performances. But what most of us don't see is the effort, trials, and failures that lead to such mastery.

The Beginning: Inspired But Afraid

My journey from being limited by fear to finding my voice was anything but smooth, and it's one that may connect with you as you face your challenges in communication and leadership. It all started with inspiration. As a boy, I was enchanted by great speakers such as Patrick Henry and Abraham Lincoln, whose words alone could inspire revolutions and change history. I wanted to be one of those people, the ones who could stand in front of crowds and not merely speak but also deeply touch lives. I experienced the power of effective communication, and I wanted to harness that mighty force.

But then reality hit. Every time I stood before a crowd to speak, my voice would betray me. Instead of commanding the room, I fumbled, stumbled, and shut down. The eloquence I admired in others seemed beyond my reach. It didn't matter how much I wanted it; desire alone wasn't enough to overcome the fear and nerves that gripped me. The moments I hoped to inspire others were marred by embarrassment and frustration.

One vivid memory stands out from my teenage years. I was the lead singer in a rock band, a context where I should have felt comfortable. Part of my role was to engage the crowd, tell stories, and introduce the songs. But even with the confidence that came from holding a microphone in my hand, I couldn't find my own words. I found someone else's words to sing songs, but when it came time for me to use my own voice, I choked, and the connection I wanted to create with the audience fell flat. It was a harsh realization that wanting something and being able to achieve it are two very different things.

Assessing Where You Are Right Now

Effective speaking is built on three core pillars: *structure, content,* and *delivery.* When I coach my clients, I start by asking them to take a moment to assess themselves in each of these areas. You can do the same now. Rate yourself on a scale of one to five in the following:

- Structure: How well do you organize your thoughts? Do you open with a bang, such as telling a story or using a provocative statement, or do you begin with something stale like, "Good afternoon, ladies and gentlemen"? Do you present ideas in a way that is easy to follow and impactful?

- Content: How compelling is your message? Are you using stories, facts, and persuasive techniques effectively? Do you repeat key phrases that become memorable in the audience's mind?

- Delivery: Do you speak with confidence, clarity, and engagement? Or do you stand behind a lectern, gripping the edges with tense hands? Are you using voice modulation, body language, and moving with purpose? Or do you speak in a monotone while pacing back and forth so the audience feels like they are watching a tennis match?

Next, ask yourself where you would like to be in six months in each of these three areas. What specific actions will you take to improve?

By the time you finish reading this book, if you apply the principles and do the exercises, you should see radical improvement. The key is intentional practice. The more you refine your structure, sharpen your content, and elevate your delivery, the closer you'll get to commanding any room with confidence and authenticity.

Why Your Voice Matters More Than Ever

Have you ever sat through a speech or presentation so dull or uninspired that you could barely stay awake? Perhaps even you have delivered such a lackluster speech. But what if your speech was your only chance to persuade an audience at a critical moment in their lives? What if, in that fleeting moment, you failed?

The truth is that most speeches are forgotten by the next day. Why is this the case? In *Made to Stick*, by Chip Heath and Dan Heath, the authors emphasize that most presentations and ideas fail to make a lasting impact because they aren't designed to "stick." Many communications, such as business presentations, don't connect with the audience due to overuse of abstract language, the "curse of knowledge," and a failure to break through common attention patterns. They highlight that sticky ideas are simple, unexpected, concrete, credible, emotional, and story-driven, which are often missing from typical presentations.[2]

John Medina discusses in his book *Brain Rules* that speeches are often soon forgotten because of how the brain processes and retains information. He explains that the human brain is not wired to handle long sessions of passive listening, which is the format of many presentations. He emphasizes the importance of engaging the brain through storytelling, visual aids, and interactive content to enhance memory and impact.[3]

Why does all this matter to you? Because you have something to say, something that can possibly change lives. Your ideas, your vision, your work—they all have the potential to make a significant impact, but only if your message touches a nerve and sticks with your audience long after you've spoken. Imagine the missed opportunities—for you, your business, your cause—when your message fails to land. Imagine the silence that follows your speech—not because you were heard, but because you were forgotten.

There is another kind of silence that comes not from lack of skill, but from fear of negative consequences. History is filled with individuals who dared to speak unpopular truths and paid a steep price. Galileo Galilei was condemned and tortured for challenging the Church's view of the universe. Edward Snowden became a global fugitive for exposing government surveillance. James Damore was fired for questioning workplace orthodoxy at Google. These weren't reckless provocateurs. They were thinkers who used reason, evidence, and logic and still faced professional exile or public vilification.

Their stories reveal a deeper, more troubling reality: That silence is often a survival strategy. It's the kind of silence that creeps in when the cost of truth is too high. Think of the geniuses whose voices were never heard because they lacked the freedom or the courage to speak out. And yet, when individuals choose to speak anyway, despite the risk, they elevate the rest of us. Every time a voice like that is silenced, it's not just their loss; it's a loss for progress, for truth, and human flourishing.

This last point was so important that philosopher John Stuart Mill covered it in his *On Liberty*: "If all mankind minus one were of one opinion, and only one person was of the contrary opinion, mankind would be no more justified in silencing that one person than he, if he had the power, would be justified in silencing mankind."[4] Mill emphasizes that silencing even one dissenting voice robs the audience of the chance to either correct their own misunderstandings or strengthen their own beliefs through debate. Blocking free speech denies people the opportunity to engage with the truth.

Another fear grips even the most confident among us. Public speaking is a common and crippling fear. We even have a term for it: glossophobia. Many have claimed that this affects up to 75 percent of the population, but some of the best studies consistently show that this fear grips 20–25 percent of the population surveyed.[5] That is a lot of people no matter which statistic is true.

Glossophobia isn't just a personal inconvenience; it's a barrier to persuading others, which makes it a barrier to your success. This fear can keep you locked in a smaller version of yourself, where your voice is muted and your impact is minimal.

Why does this happen? Why do so many of us freeze up, our voices shrinking to whispers when we need them to roar? We'll explore different aspects of fear that contribute to these limitations.

There's more at stake than your message just being remembered. In today's world, your freedom to speak, to express your ideas, and to engage with others is increasingly under threat. But the freedom to communicate isn't a luxury only for public figures. It's a fundamental right, built into the US Constitution. From boardrooms to courtrooms, the ability to speak freely affects how we lead, influence, and live. *That's where the connection between liberty and leadership comes in.*

Even if you don't deliberately promote liberty in a political forum, in every structured or unstructured communication, you rely on the freedom to speak your mind, the freedom to express what matters to you. When you lose that freedom, either through external pressure or internal fear, your effectiveness as a leader diminishes. The greatest leaders, whether they are entrepreneurs, executives, or intellectuals, understand that their voice is their main tool of influence.

This brings us to the two primary groups who struggle with speaking effectively.

People Who Fear Speaking

These are individuals who avoid public speaking or delivering presentations altogether because of one or more of the following fears:

- They believe they have nothing important to say: They assume their ideas lack value when, in fact, it's usually just a sign they haven't taken the time to think clearly and organize their thoughts.

- They fear public embarrassment: The thought of being laughed at or ridiculed haunts and paralyzes them.

- They fear being criticized: The anxiety of being judged or misunderstood keeps them silent.

- They don't know enough about their topic: A lack of confidence in their knowledge makes them hesitant.

- They have a speech impediment that serves as an obstacle: Physical limitations and/or past trauma create barriers.

People Who Speak Fearfully

These individuals do speak, but their effectiveness is hampered by specific fears:

- Fear of speaking freely or saying what they really think: They self-censor because potential consequences—job loss, assassination, or other harm—loom large.

- Fear of being forgotten: They worry their message will not have a lasting impact.

- Fear of being misunderstood: They fear that their message may be unclear or misconstrued, potentially causing them or their ideas to be mischaracterized.

- Fear of being heckled and losing focus: The possibility of confrontation or losing their train of thought makes them risk-averse.

- Fear of stating the obvious and being ignored: They dread that their message may be considered redundant or irrelevant.

These fears, whether they keep you from speaking at all or diminish the impact of your words, are significant barriers to your potential. Together, they create a perfect storm that can hinder even the most capable individuals, shrinking not only your voice but also your character and your potential.

Economic and psychological costs come from poor verbal communication skills. One study found that after three days, a user retained only 10 to 20 percent of spoken information, but almost 65 percent of visual information.[6] Also, according to David Grossman, poor communication increases employee turnover, decreases engagement, and reduces performance. The cost for companies with one hundred thousand or more employees was $37 billion annually.[7] Think of what these numbers could mean for your business.

Do you often avoid speaking or hold yourself back when you do speak, when you know you have something important to say, more to give, more to achieve? *Is this how you want to live?* It doesn't have to be this way.

This book is your guide to breaking out of bondage and finding freedom. It's about reclaiming or finding your voice, mastering the art of communication, and generating the full power of your potential. It's about learning and using the tools and strategies that can transform your ability to speak, to lead, and to inspire. It's about creating an environment where your ideas can flourish, and where your voice is not just heard, but remembered.

Consider this: Every day, you make countless choices, often without realizing their significance. These choices, small as they seem, shape your character and life. But what happens when those choices are taken away?

What happens when your right to speak, to choose your words, to engage with others freely, is stripped from you? That's not just a loss of freedom; it's life under tyranny.

And make no mistake, tyranny doesn't always come in obvious forms. It can be subtle, creeping in through the fear of judgment, the pressure to conform, the silence imposed by those who would prefer you to stay quiet, or the silence you impose on yourself for fear of punishment. In her book *No Apologies*, Katherine Brodsky coins an expression for this phenomenon: the "silenced majority."[8]

Voices of Reason is a call to action. It's about recognizing the immense value of your voice and the profound impact you can have when you use it effectively. It's about moving beyond fears—fear of speaking, fear of losing your freedom, fear of being forgotten—and embracing the responsibility and the privilege of being heard.

It's time to break free from the chains that have held you back. It's time to actualize the potential that lies within you. *Your voice matters.* It's time to make sure the world knows it. This journey starts now.

CHAPTER 2

The Blueprint For Finding Your Voice

"Let rhetoric, then, be a power of seeing what is capable of being persuasive on each subject."
—ARISTOTLE[1]

L ike many steps on one's quest for excellence, the pathway to becoming a powerful speaker does not proceed in a straight line. There is some progress, then apparent regress, where effort doesn't necessarily generate results. Nevertheless, one tries to keep moving forward.

Here are some highlights from my own odyssey from fumbling for words onstage to owning the stage with confidence and becoming a professional speaking coach.

The Turning Point: A Quest For Excellence

Once I left rock music to become a global data center manager at Merrill Lynch, clear communication became even more crucial. Imagine stock traders unable to trade due to technical failures, and you are the one responsible for fixing it fast. You need an authoritative voice. Yet, I wasn't a drill sergeant. Past verbal failures—stumbling over words in school, freezing on stage, fumbling in job interviews—haunted me. Fear of disapproval, misunderstanding, and even ridicule gnawed at my confidence.

Leadership became my testing ground. If I wanted to be a powerful speaker and a trusted leader, I had to master communication. I enrolled in a Dale Carnegie public speaking course culminating in a speech contest. Winning it was a breakthrough, teaching me that fear can be managed and even turned into an asset.

In 1992, I joined Toastmasters International, where I practiced, received feedback, and refined my style. Over the years, I pursued further training, earning a World Class Speaking Coach certification under World Champion speaker Craig Valentine. It was about more than just speaking well; it was about purpose, passion, and impact.

Today, I'm an active member of Darren LaCroix's Stage Time University and Craig Valentine's Speak and Prosper Academy, continually refining my craft. Thanks to coaching mentors such as Ford Saeks, Chris McGuire, Sam Richter, and many others, I now get paid to speak and coach, incorporating storytelling, humor, and structured techniques I once lacked. (I also gained great value from Brian Johnson's Heroic program, Donald Miller's Small Business Flight School, and Benjamin Hardy's Rapid Transformation.)

When I lead group coaching sessions, I start by describing what's in it for the attendees. I share a quotation from *Deliver Unforgettable Presentations*, by Patricia Fripp, Darren LaCroix, and Mark Brown: "Developing good public speaking skills is the best way to promote your product, service, or company."[2]

Going from fear to confidence to mastery has been long and arduous for me, but it has also been incredibly rewarding. Not only have I improved my own communication skills, but I have experienced the joy of helping others turn their fear into confidence when speaking before a group. You'll learn about several success stories in chapters 3 through 9.

Breaking Through To Become A Voice Of Reason

In the mid-1990s, I took on the daunting challenge of hosting and producing a Manhattan cable TV show, *The Voice of Reason*, which explored how reason shapes a richer, fuller, happier life. Each week, I crafted an opening script, fine-tuned my delivery, and studied great hosts like Tom Snyder and Lou Rukeyser. I learned to think critically, engage guests, and adapt on the spot.

One defining moment came before my first episode on education. A guest asked whether we could edit out mistakes, and I responded, "No, we record in one take. Just like *Saturday Night Live*." The experience forced me to stay sharp, respond quickly, and own my own words. Walking past the Flatiron Building after a show one evening, I realized: I love this, and I'm good at it.

I learned that mastering communication isn't about eliminating fear but about channeling it productively. The best communicators combine logic, emotional connection, and moral clarity. Looking back on those recordings reminds me how far I've come.

Founding The New York Heroes Society: Celebrating Leadership And Liberty

As my speaking and leadership skills grew, I sought to celebrate the values that shaped my journey: leadership, personal freedom, and liberty. In 2004, I founded the New York Heroes Society, honoring leaders who championed these ideals.

One of the most fulfilling aspects was leading walking tours of NYC's liberty monuments, from George Washington to William Tecumseh

Sherman to Ulysses S. Grant. These were more than history lessons; they were immersive experiences in the ideals that shaped my own path.

I also led twice-yearly hikes up mountains near West Point, such as Breakneck Ridge and Bear Mountain. At the summit, participants engaged in a "celebrate self" segment where they publicly shared achievements and goals while honing presentation skills. It was about breaking barriers, embracing challenges, and inspiring growth. The New York Heroes Society became a real-world test of my speaking philosophy. I wasn't just preaching my ideas; I was living them and helping others find their voice, just as I had found mine.

Aristotle's Blueprint: Ethos, Logos, Pathos

A key turning point for me came when I reengaged with history's first voice of reason: Aristotle. I had first discovered Aristotle's works as a teenager. Much of it flew over my head and a lot of it still does today, despite currently being in my eighth year of doing a deep dive into all of his works. However, three of his principles have stayed with me from the beginning: his idea that happiness (which he called eudaemonia) is the ultimate purpose of life; his emphasis on the value of friendship; and his insistence on the importance of reasoning, that is, reaching conclusions based on evidence and logic.

Aristotle's seminal work on persuasion, *Rhetoric*, became the foundation of my speaking and coaching practice. He states, "Let rhetoric, then, be a power of seeing what is capable of being persuasive on each subject."[3]

This definition emphasizes that rhetoric is about more than just speaking well. It's also about finding the best way to persuade a particular audience in a given situation. Aristotle believed rhetoric was necessary for engaging and convincing others, whether in politics, law, or everyday life.

In modern usage, "rhetoric" often refers to something negative, such as when people say, "That's just rhetoric." What they usually mean is "that's nonsense" or "that's fancy fluff." Aristotle disagreed, and one of my goals in this book is to restore the positive connotation that the term rhetoric deserves.

At the heart of Aristotle's blueprint are *ethos, logos*, and *pathos*, the three pillars of persuasion. When used skillfully, these elements create messages that stick and endure over time. Let's look at each pillar.

Ethos: Character And Credibility

Ethos is about establishing the speaker's moral character. Aristotle believed that people are more likely to be persuaded by someone they trust: combined with being an authority on the subject at hand, moral character establishes credibility and trust. He explained, "Persuasion is by means of character whenever the speech is spoken in such a way as to make the speaker trustworthy."[4] This means that a speaker's credibility is about the content of one's speech as well as how the speaker presents themself and their reputation. Ethos involves demonstrating trustworthiness, authority, and integrity on the subject at hand.

An authority is someone who possesses expertise, experience, and knowledge in a particular subject. This expertise can be developed through education, experience, or success in each field. Aristotle recognized that authority is about knowledge, which means demonstrating wisdom and practical judgment. He stated, "For we are more persuaded, and more quickly, by decent people, about all matters without exception and completely so in matters in which there is nothing precise but there is divided opinion."[5] In other words, people are naturally inclined to trust those who have both knowledge and a proven record of sound judgment.

How does a speaker establish authority? Demonstrating experience or credentials and citing relevant background, education, or achievements helps solidify expertise. This is done by using clear, confident communication; speaking with clarity and assurance reinforces credibility.

Integrity refers to the consistency among a person's words, values, and actions. Someone with integrity doesn't merely say what is right and good but also acts in alignment with their stated belief. Aristotle emphasized that trustworthiness is essential for persuasion: "But character, one might say, has in it just about the most decisive means of persuasion."[6] This means that audiences are more likely to accept a speaker's message when they believe them to be honest and ethical.

Integrity in communication involves avoiding deception (honesty), aligning words with actions over time (consistency), and respect for the audience by showing goodwill, ensuring the message serves the audience's best interest.

Aristotle continues by speaking about the moral standing of a speaker (honor) and the credibility in the form of reputation: "Honor and good reputation are among the most pleasant things, because they make everyone imagine that he is the sort of person who has serious stature, and more so when he believes the people who say so are telling the truth."[7] Here, he reinforces the idea that the speaker's influence is deeply tied to their ethical standing and public perception. By consistently upholding character and earning the respect of others, a speaker can command attention and belief, making their words more impactful. A speaker establishes moral character not by declaring virtue, but by embodying it through integrity in speech, authenticity in presence, and respect for the audience's mind.

In summary, ethos is built on character and credibility, and these two qualities determine whether an audience trusts a speaker. Character reflects moral virtue, which is the speaker's goodness, justice, courage, and honesty. It also includes good judgment (which Aristotle termed *phronesis*), the wisdom to make sound decisions, and goodwill, showing thoughtfulness, respect, and genuine concern for the audience. A speaker who embodies these traits earns moral authority.

Credibility comes from expertise, experience, and education, which means a speaker's authority on a subject. But credibility also demands integrity: meaning what you say, doing what you promise, and speaking with sincerity. When these elements combine, they create trust, the foundation of all persuasion.

Aristotle makes it clear that persuasion relies on logical argument (logos) and emotional appeal (pathos), but most importantly, on the speaker's ability to embody the virtues that make them believable, respectable, and worth listening to.

Personal Insight

The importance of ethos in my life cannot be overstated. Early on, I learned that trust is a currency that is just as valuable as knowledge or skill. My transition from being a front man in a rock band to managing a team at Merrill Lynch and eventually becoming the founder of the New York Heroes Society and of Speaking With Purpose LLC depended on my ability to build trust with those around me. As a manager, I had to earn the trust of my team, where mistakes cost stock traders (and the business) millions of dollars per minute. My team needed to see that I understood the challenges we faced and that I embodied the principles I promoted, such as integrity, accountability, and a commitment to success.

Ethos is more than just being trustworthy; it's about consistently aligning your words with your actions. Speakers who lack credibility will not be persuasive, no matter how logically or emotionally compelling their argument may be.

In my coaching, I often encounter clients who struggle with establishing ethos in their professional roles. This usually happens when they only focus on the content of their ideas, a mistake I often made during my early years as a speaker. Whether they are new leaders or experienced executives, they eventually find that if their audience doubts their sincerity, their message will fall flat. I help them focus on how to communicate their values clearly, ensuring that their audience sees them as both knowledgeable and principled.

As a speaker, I have also found that building trust with an audience means sharing personal stories that reflect my principles, which reinforces my ethos through both speech and action. This also comes from maintaining eye contact instead of staring at my notes or at a PowerPoint screen behind me.

Logos: Logical Argument

Aristotle emphasized the importance of logic in persuasion, claiming that a speaker must present arguments that are sound, consistent, and well-supported by evidence. He stated, "And persuasion is by means of speech whenever we show something that is true, or appears so, from things that are persuasive on each subject."[8] This means that an argument must be rational as well as structured in a way that makes it compelling and relevant to the audience.

To Aristotle, logos involves the use of facts, data, and reasoning to support your argument. He stressed that logical appeal should be consistent, meaning that point A should not contradict point B. A well-constructed speech follows a clear progression of ideas, guiding the audience to a logical conclusion.

A persuasive and credible statement gains its strength in one of two ways: either it is immediately clear and self-evident, or it gains support from other well-established facts. This approach underlies the power of logical argumentation, where each point builds on the previous one, creating a structured progression that naturally leads the audience to accept the speaker's conclusion.[9]

Personal Insight

In my professional life, logos has been an essential tool, particularly in discussions about liberty and personal freedom. As the founder of the New York Heroes Society, I often led discussions on the philosophical underpinnings of liberty. These discussions weren't merely about stirring people's emotions. They were also rooted in well-constructed arguments that demonstrated how personal freedom leads to a flourishing society. The clarity and strength of these logical arguments were what persuaded many participants to take the discussions seriously.

I frequently remind my coaching clients how important logical reasoning is to a successful presentation. No matter how passionate or compelling a speaker might be, their argument is weak without logos.

When I coach individuals on crafting their speeches, I emphasize the importance of constructing a clear, logical argument. This means organizing the speech following a natural progression, using evidence to support each point, and ensuring that each argument leads naturally to the next.

For example, in one keynote about the American dream, I don't just assert that liberty leads to prosperity when I speak about the benefits of liberty. I support that claim with historical examples, such as the contrast between the US and Cuba, data, and logical reasoning. I'll bring up the number of people who are starving in Cuba and risking their lives (often dying) to make it to the freer, more prosperous United States, in their pursuit of the American dream. This approach both strengthens my argument and enhances my credibility as a speaker.

Pathos: Emotional Appeal

Aristotle knew that effective persuasion requires more than just credibility and logic. It also demands a deep emotional connection between the speaker and the audience. He noted, "Persuasion is by means of the hearers, whenever they are led on into passion by the speech, for we do not render our judgments the same way when grieved as when delighted, or when friendly as when hostile."[10] This passage highlights two key aspects of pathos: the role of emotions in shaping judgment and the necessity of understanding the audience's emotional state.

But his insight goes further. Many people misunderstand pathos as simply creating an emotional connection between the speaker and the audience. However, Aristotle presents a more nuanced view: pathos is fundamentally about understanding what the audience cares about and how to move them into a particular emotional state.

He explains, "And it is evident that, by one's speech, one might need to prepare people to be of the same sort as those feeling prone to anger, and to present one's opponents as guilty of those things which cause people to get angry and as being the sort of people they get angry at."[11] This highlights the speaker's role both in stirring emotion and in shaping and directing it toward a specific rhetorical purpose.

Let's elaborate on this: Aristotle understood that audiences do not enter a speech with a blank emotional state. They come with preexisting emotions, biases, and inclinations. A skilled speaker must assess the audience's emotional disposition before attempting to shift it. This means understanding what the audience already feels about a topic, which events or experiences trigger certain emotions in them, and which desired emotional state will make them more receptive to persuasion.

Aristotle recognized that emotions play a huge role in shaping judgment, but also believed they needed to be guided by reason and moral character. His approach to pathos was about understanding the audience's emotional state and using that knowledge to lead them to a rational conclusion.

At this point, you might wonder: "Isn't this just manipulation?" The short answer is: it depends. In Aristotle's time, a group of traveling teachers, the sophists, took a very different approach to persuasion. They focused almost entirely on emotional appeal, using rhetorical tricks to win arguments *without concern for truth or ethics*. Their goal wasn't to guide an audience toward wisdom and justice, but simply to persuade them by whatever means necessary—whether flattery, fear, or deception.

Aristotle strongly opposed this approach. In fact, one of the reasons he wrote *Rhetoric* was to correct the way people viewed persuasion. He believed that a great speaker should combine character and credibility (ethos), logic (logos), and emotion (pathos) in a balanced way. If a speaker only appeals to emotion without the foundation of reason, that speaker is no better than a sophist, using persuasion as a tool for manipulation rather than truth.

So, Aristotle wasn't against emotional appeals, he just believed they should be tied to moral character and argument. His version of pathos is about more than just stirring emotions—it's about guiding them toward a deeper understanding of truth and why they should care about it.

Personal Insight

In my own life and work, I've seen how pathos can transform a speech by creating a meaningful connection between the speaker and the audience by tapping into shared experiences, values, and aspirations. During our biannual hikes with the New York Heroes Society, this principle came to life in a powerful way.

One of the key elements of pathos is setting the right context to enhance emotional resonance. In these hikes, the environment itself played a role in shaping emotions. The changing seasons, the vibrant colors of autumn, or the fresh spring bloom mirrored the themes of personal growth, perseverance, and renewal. Nature became a metaphor for the highs and lows of life, reinforcing the stories people shared.

Beyond the setting, the structure of the hikes encouraged emotional connection. By stopping to reflect on personal victories and challenges during what we called "celebrate self," participants built a sense of shared humanity. When someone joyously announced a major achievement, like publishing a book, the group celebrated together. Similarly, they shared the weight of difficult moments, like when my dear friend Bruce Rickard courageously announced his terminal illness. These moments weren't simply emotional; they created a deep bond, making each individual feel heard, valued, and connected to something amazing.

In public speaking, context is everything when it comes to pathos. A speech delivered in a boardroom may land very differently than one delivered in the outdoors. The Heroes hikes amplified the impact of personal storytelling by blending physical movement, a natural setting, and an open forum for heartfelt expression.

By understanding an audience's emotional needs and framing the experience in a way that enhances connection, a speaker can create both a speech and an unforgettable moment of shared meaning. (One caveat: In chapter 6, we'll analyze the damage caused by speakers who rely *only* on emotional appeal.)

In my coaching practice, I often work with clients to find the emotional core of their message. What personal stories can they share that will connect with their audience? How can they frame their message in a way that speaks to the hopes, fears, and desires of the people they are addressing? Pathos, when used effectively, makes a message unforgettable.

Future Indian diplomat and philosophy student Walter Sylesh had some thoughts to share after he heard my Voices of Reason presentation in Nairobi, Kenya:

> Aristotle's Art of Rhetoric changed how I look at speeches. Over the years, as I gained confidence on speaking coherently in public, I wondered what made some speeches great and stand out. My early years and limited exposure urged me to consider speeches by any US president or world leader to be admirable. The very fact that someone could go on stage and address a huge crowd was my benchmark (which comes primarily from ethos). But now, with the Voices of Reason and my deeper understanding of the principles of what makes human society flourish, I began to evaluate speeches using the Triad: Is the speech credible, coherent as well as captivating? The "3 Cs" are a more reliable benchmark for me, differentiating a great speech from an ordinary, logical, or popular one.[12]

Walter is one of my clients who found his voice, gained confidence in speaking, and learned how to apply Aristotle's principles of rhetoric to verbal communication.

The Solution: Tools And Atmosphere For Success

Early on, I discovered that to speak and lead effectively, we need the right tools and the right atmosphere. By this, I mean creating an environment that allows for open and effective communication. In the context of public speaking and leadership, having the right atmosphere is about fostering spaces where individuals feel comfortable expressing their thoughts without fear of retribution, but also with constructive feedback from a communication expert. This is crucial for both personal and professional growth.

Supportive Environment

Just like in Toastmasters, the environment needs to be supportive and structured for growth. People need to feel they can fail without severe consequences. However, they also need to receive encouraging, constructive feedback and then use that feedback to improve.

Freedom To Experiment

To communicate effectively, individuals must be able to experiment with different styles of presentation and storytelling. (For those bold enough to try it, I recommend improv classes.) This experimentation is only possible in an atmosphere that values creativity and resilience over perfection.

Toward that end, I founded Speaking With Purpose LLC, where our goal is to cultivate an enlightened environment that goes beyond just the immediate support of individuals. It promotes an atmosphere where ideas, products, and services can flourish through freedom of expression and exchange of thoughts.

Examples include a value-driven culture of openness with an encouraging growth mindset. The openness allows for different perspectives and intellectual diversity. The values of integrity and benevolence drive discussion and debates centered around reasoned arguments (logos), they respect the character and experience of others (ethos), and they appeal to common values and shared emotional experiences (pathos).

Our focus on growth over fixed traits turns mistakes into learning opportunities instead of setbacks. In the context of Speaking With Purpose LLC, this means participants are not just coached to give a good speech; they are also encouraged to cultivate a mindset of continuous improvement. This pursuit of excellence is embraced, with failures seen as stepping stones toward greater confidence.

In other words, I help others develop voices of reason and lead the charge for their own liberty. This book is about giving you those tools and helping you create that atmosphere for yourself and those around you.

Introducing The Process

Now that you know the path I took and the principles that guided me, let me share the process I developed to help others achieve similar success. This process is built on the foundation of Aristotle's blueprint—ethos, logos, and pathos—and refined through my experiences coaching individuals from diverse backgrounds and skill levels.

Here's how it works:

- Identify the core fears and challenges: The first step is to understand what holds individuals back from effective communication. It's about acknowledging the fears that hinder one's expression. (As an aside, Aristotle identified courage as a cardinal virtue in his *Nicomachean Ethics*, but that's the subject for another book.)

- Apply Aristotle's blueprint (ethos, logos, pathos): These three pillars build a foundation for persuasive communication.

- Use real-world application through historical examples: By learning from great orators and historical moments, individuals can understand how to apply ethos, logos, and pathos in their own communication.

- Utilize customized coaching and continuous support: Providing one-on-one guidance that caters to each person's unique needs ensures they continue to grow and refine their skills.

- Focus on the long-term impact: Finally, this process isn't about short-term gains. It's about creating lasting change and giving individuals the confidence and tools to continue growing as communicators and leaders.

This combination of the right tools, the right atmosphere, and a well-defined process ensures that individuals can find and use their voice effectively, ultimately making an impact in their personal and professional lives.

A Journey From Fear To Legacy

This book will give you the power to find the courage to tell others what you really believe, and they will respect you for how you communicate your ideas. It will empower you to find the ability to say precisely what you mean instead of feeling inarticulate. It will enable you to overcome your fears and let others take you seriously with your words.

You will learn that fears, setbacks, and failures are all part of the quest, but they don't define it. What defines the quest is how you respond and grow from them, and how you use what you've learned to leave a lasting legacy.

In chapters 3 through 9, we'll explore the achievements of those who have come before us: great speakers, thinkers, and leaders who, like you, faced their own challenges and fears. The "magnificent seven," who are the seven historical figures whose speeches we'll analyze, are not an exhaustive list; they are speeches that have had a significant impact on me personally. Some of those speakers paid a steep price for their courage. We'll see how those speakers used their voices to change the world, and how you can do the same in your own way.

Chapters 10 and 11 describe how to sustain your effort as you go into the future.

By the end of this book, you'll have the tools you need to speak effectively and understand how to use your voice to lead, inspire, and create the impact you were meant to have.

Going from fear to comfort to excellence is difficult, but it's worth it. It has taken me years to walk this path, and I have stumbled often and still do so, though much less nowadays. As my speaking coach Craig Valentine says, "Let my long road become your shortcut." Together, we'll break the chains that might be holding you back, so that you can discover the full potential of your voice and the power it has to change your life and the lives of those around you.

PART II

Lessons From Liberty's Leaders

CHAPTER 3

An Enlightenment Voice Of Reason

"These are the times that try men's souls."
—THOMAS PAINE[1]

By applying Aristotle's blueprint—ethos, logos, and pathos—you can transform your ability to persuade. Instead of stumbling over words or losing your audience, you'll command the room. Your message will stick, and your ideas will move people.

Don't worry if this feels too new to apply right away; through examples provided in chapters 3 through 9, you'll learn to spot this formula in your sleep.

We'll now move from the ancient world, where Cicero, deeply influenced by Aristotle's *Rhetoric*, was hailed as a master of the spoken word, to the Age of Enlightenment and the birth of the United States of America.

The Struggle For Liberty And Justice

In the 1760s and 1770s, the British-American colonists considered themselves proud, loyal British subjects. Some, such as George Washington, had helped Britain defeat the French in the Seven Years' War. The colonists wanted continued self-government, with little interference from a tiny island across the Atlantic Ocean called England. However, little by little, they experienced the violation of their individual "rights of Englishmen."

The colonists didn't rebel overnight. First came the Stamp Act, which taxed everything from newspapers to legal documents, without giving them a voice in Parliament. Then the Quartering Act allowed British soldiers to sleep in their homes—no invitation needed. The Intolerable Acts cracked down on free speech and local government. The Quebec Act raised alarms by favoring Catholicism in nearby Canada—many Protestants feared their religious freedom was next. The Massachusetts Government Act tightened British control and made it difficult for colonists to defend themselves by limiting town meetings and disarming them. If they protested, they could be shipped off to Britain for trial. And, when Boston's harbor was shut down through the Boston Port Act, economic lifelines were cut. Still, many colonists—Loyalists—chose submission over resistance, no matter how tyrannical the rule became.

It is in this context that we find the first formal, public speech that called for American independence. On March 23, 1775, Patrick Henry walked into St. John's Church in Richmond, Virginia, packed with attendees of the Second Virginia Convention. One decade earlier, he earned a reputation for pushing the envelope publicly by protesting the 1765 Stamp Act. When Henry was interrupted by calls of "Treason! Treason!" he calmly replied, "If this be treason, make the most of it."[2] This kind of political rebellion was unheard of in the New World.

After listening to other speakers in St. John's Church, Henry rose and spoke about the illusion of hope. With mounting intensity, he concluded with words that would forever shake the American colonies and set the stage for a revolutionary war: "Give me liberty, or give me death."[3]

Henry's rousing speech dramatizes the power of rhetorical excellence in mobilizing people toward a common goal, even in the face of overwhelming odds. He demonstrated the principles of effective communication, ethical leadership, and passionate defense of liberty using ethos, logos, and pathos.

Ethos: Establishing Credibility

Henry begins by respecting his opponents when he says, "No man thinks more highly than I do of the patriotism, as well as abilities, of the very worthy gentlemen who have just addressed the house."[4] This opening serves an important ethical purpose. By recognizing the integrity of those who disagree with him, Henry establishes himself as fair-minded and respectful, which increases his credibility by showing goodwill toward those he disagrees with. Instead of dismissing or attacking his opponents outright, he demonstrates that he values their commitment to their country. This shows that his argument is not driven by personal hostility but by a genuine concern for the liberty of all.

Additionally, this tactic disarms resistance from his audience. When people feel respected, they are more likely to listen rather than react defensively. Henry's use of goodwill sets the stage for a more persuasive appeal, making it more difficult for his opponents to dismiss him as radical or reckless.

This approach reflects one of Aristotle's key principles of ethos: that a speaker must appear virtuous and reasonable to be persuasive. By showing that he is not driven by personal animosity but by principle, Henry strengthens his moral authority and makes his call to action more compelling.

Henry goes on to show his commitment to the truth: "For my own part, whatever anguish of spirit it may cost, I am willing to know the whole truth; to know the worst, and to provide for it."[5] By showing himself as a truth seeker, regardless of the personal cost, he bolsters his moral character, which makes it more likely that his ideas will persuade others.

Having previously been accused of treason by some of those same people in the room, Henry heightens the conflict: "Should I keep back my opinions at such a time, through fear of giving offense, I should consider myself as guilty of treason toward my country."[6] Henry builds his credibility by presenting himself as someone unafraid to confront reality, no matter how harsh. This statement reinforces his commitment to honesty and courage, showing he does not seek to evade uncomfortable facts.

This lets his audience know he is not afraid to speak. More importantly, aligning his actions with his thoughts signals his integrity and moral courage. This helps persuade his listeners that he is not only speaking from principles, but that his own life and future are at stake.

Logos: Using Logical Arguments

Henry builds his argument for armed resistance through a logical structure based on experience and principle. He states: "I have but one lamp by which my feet are guided, and that is the lamp of experience."[7]

By using experience as his guide, Henry grounds his argument in observable reality rather than wishful thinking. He appeals to the audience's shared knowledge of British actions over the past decade, urging them to assess the situation logically rather than to rely on false hope that Britain will change its approach.

Henry presents a series of rhetorical questions that force his audience to logically connect past British actions to their likely future consequences: "I ask, gentlemen, sir, what means this martial array, if its purpose be not to force us to submission? Can gentlemen assign any other possible motive for it?"[8] Here, Henry is making a deductive argument:

Premise one: Britain has sent fleets and armies to the colonies.

Premise two: Military force is used to compel obedience, not reconciliation.

Conclusion: The British are preparing to subjugate, not negotiate.

Henry's use of logical reasoning makes it clear that continuing peaceful dialogue is futile. His argument is not based on speculation; it's a conclusion drawn from the facts of British aggression.

Once he establishes that British rule is not open to reform, Henry shifts to the central principle at stake: freedom versus slavery. He states: "For my own part, I consider it as nothing less than a question of freedom or slavery."[9]

This framing eliminates any middle ground. Henry presents only two possible outcomes: either the colonists resist British oppression and secure their *freedom*, or they submit and accept *slavery* under an unaccountable government. This either-or framing forces the audience to view the situation with moral clarity. They must act or they will be complicit in their own subjugation.

Henry then reinforces his logic by addressing common counterarguments. Some in the audience may believe the colonies should wait for better conditions before fighting. Henry refutes this by asking: "They tell us, sir, that we are weak; unable to cope with so formidable an adversary. But when will we be stronger? Will it be the next week, or the next year?"[10]

This rhetorical question exposes the irrationality of waiting. By asking when they will be stronger, Henry challenges his audience to find a rational justification for delay. Since no future conditions guarantee strength, the logical conclusion is that they must take action now.

Henry's entire logical case for resistance is built upon two pillars: experience and principle. Experience shows that Britain has consistently used force and deception rather than negotiation. Principle dictates that submission equals slavery, and liberty is worth defending.

By combining historical evidence with moral reasoning, Henry's speech persuades many in his audience that resistance is not an option. It is a necessity.

Pathos: Stirring Emotional Response

Henry's speech stirs the emotions greatly, not only with his words but also with his delivery style, which amplifies the impact of his message. He effectively raises fear and urgency: "There is no retreat but in submission and slavery! Our chains are forged! Their clanking may be heard on the plains of Boston! The war is inevitable—and let it come! I repeat it, sir, let it come."[11] Henry paints a terrifying picture of the colonists already in bondage, evoking a sense of impending doom. His use of vivid imagery—"chains" and "clanking"—stirs fear and dread in his audience.

As Henry delivered this line, it was reported that his voice rose, giving a sense of inevitability. Also, by repeating "let it come," he emphasizes the emotional force behind his acceptance of war, driving the point home through sheer intensity. In *A Son of Thunder*, Henry Mayer describes the impact of this sentence: "He let the words float in the air for a long time, and when the silence grew nearly unbearable, he made them echo. 'Let it come!!'"[12]

Another emotional appeal is to his audience's sense of honor: "Is life so dear, or peace so sweet, as to be purchased at the price of chains and slavery?"[13] Here, he questions the audience about whether they value life and peace enough to pay the price of losing their liberty. The contrast between "peace" and "chains and slavery" taps into the emotions of pride, fear, and shame. Henry's delivery style demonstrated a slow, deliberate pace, allowing the gravity of each word—"life," "peace," "chains," "slavery"—to sink in. His tone rose as he built toward the ultimate question of what is truly worth living for.

Henry reaches an emotional peak, concluding with his famous declaration: "I know not what course others may take, but as for me, give me liberty, or give me death!" This final line is one of the most emotionally charged sentences in American history. Henry presents an either-or choice: freedom or death. He values liberty so much that he's prepared to die for it. This dramatic, passionate appeal stirs deep emotions of bravery and determination.

In this climactic moment, as described by Henry Mayer, Patrick Henry "had paused, arms flung outward, as the word 'liberty' rang out in the hushed sanctuary; then he smote his breast with an imaginary dagger in the perfect embodiment of heroic Roman virtue."[14] Henry's voice was filled with passion, showing the heightened conflict in a final choice. The physical delivery conjured in the minds of his audience well-known historical images of heroic freedom fighters.

Henry's delivery was truly a performance. His use of a rising voice created a sense of urgency, his pauses allowed the audience to digest the weight of his words, and his gestures (from bondage to arms raised in freedom) turned his words into a visual spectacle that amplified the emotional force of his message.

Using both pathos and performance made Henry's speech not only a series of well-formed arguments but also an emotional experience to stir his audience to action. His mastery of the spoken word, both in content and delivery, made "Give me liberty, or give me death" one of the most stirring calls to arms in history. His passionate plea for the cause of liberty struck a deep chord with his listeners, moving them to act. And act they did.

The Lasting Impact Of Words

In *Patrick Henry: Champion of Liberty*, author Jon Kukla describes the stunned silence after Henry finished, which was only broken by a seventeen-year-old enlisted colonial soldier named Edward Carrington who spoke up. He was standing near the window outside of the church and said: "'Let me be buried at this spot . . .' Some thirty-five years later, his family honored that request. Now, after two and a half centuries, his grave bears witness to the speech that burned itself into the memory of countless listeners."[15] I went to that site many times when I visited Richmond in order to pay tribute to Carrington, who was so deeply moved by Henry's words.

Also in attendance was George Washington, who took up the call "To arms!" and would lead the Continental Army to ultimate victory. Five of the six Virginia signers of the *Declaration of Independence* were present and were impressed and moved by Henry's passionate message of liberty.

In Ron Chernow's biography of Alexander Hamilton, he describes how in August 1776, in New York City, twenty-one-year-old college student and artillery captain Hamilton started drilling cadets. The unit wore uniforms with caps that had stitching that described what they were fighting for: "Liberty or Death."[16] You know your message is memorable when it becomes a motto on a hat.

Overcoming Common Fears

Henry's "Give Me Liberty" speech provides enduring lessons for overcoming three common fears: the fear of public speaking, the fear of speaking freely, and the fear of being forgotten.

Fear Of Public Speaking

Lesson: Henry's ability to deliver a persuasive and commanding speech in front of the Second Virginia Convention is a perfect model in overcoming stage fright. Facing a room of seasoned politicians—many of whom were hesitant to declare independence from Britain—Henry used his voice and demeanor to command attention. He didn't rely on flowery words or unnecessary formality, but projected conviction through clear, direct language like: "The war is inevitable—and let it come! I repeat it, sir, let it come!"

Henry's confidence didn't stem from arrogance but preparation. He understood the stakes of the moment, giving him the courage to speak from the heart. This moral clarity allowed him to focus not on the fear of judgment, but on the urgency of his message.

Application

- **Preparation as armor:** Just as Henry prepared his arguments to match the gravity of the moment, modern speakers can calm nerves by mastering their material. Know your subject inside out.

- **Harness body language:** Henry stood tall, his gestures reinforcing his words. Similarly, focus on open body language: Maintain eye contact and use deliberate gestures to radiate confidence.

- **Anchor your purpose:** Reframe nervous energy as excitement. Believing in the importance of your message will inspire you and resonate with your audience.

Exercise

Record yourself delivering a key idea. Watch to identify whether your body language signals lack of confidence in your message. Adjust and refine until conviction comes naturally and can be seen and heard by your audience.

Fear Of Speaking Freely

Lesson: Henry was fully aware of the risks involved in his revolutionary rhetoric. To openly call for resistance against British rule was to invite further accusations of treason. Despite these stakes, Henry's speech pulled no punches: "I know not what course others may take; but as for me, give me liberty, or give me death!"

Henry faced not just social ostracism, but also potential imprisonment or execution. Yet his words, driven by a moral conviction in the ideals of liberty, transcended fear. Henry recognized that speaking freely was essential for change, even when it carried potentially dire consequences.

Application

- **Moral backbone:** Align your message with deeply held beliefs. When speaking freely, conviction becomes your shield. Henry's courage stemmed from the moral clarity of his cause; similarly, stay true to your core values.

- **Calculate the risks but act anyway:** Evaluate the potential backlash of speaking freely, but weigh it against the cost of silence. Henry knew that silence in the face of tyranny was more dangerous than his words. Of course, your context may be different, and others might be harmed by you speaking out. So you will need to do your own calculation when weighing the costs and benefits of speaking up for your values.

- **In practice:** Imagine a high-stakes work scenario where expressing dissent could be risky. Role-play crafting your argument in a way that shows integrity while balancing that with tact.

Exercise

Write a "redline speech" outlining something you're afraid to speak about openly. Share it in a safe environment (e.g., with a mentor) to practice both delivery and courage.

Fear Of Being Forgotten

Lesson: One reason Henry's speech has endured for centuries is his extraordinary delivery, infused with pathos. His plea for liberty wasn't just logical but also visceral, touching hearts through evocative imagery and rhythm. His final line became immortal not just because of its content, but also because of its passion.

Henry's dramatic climax likely included a deliberate pause before delivering his famous line, ensuring its emotional weight. He spoke as though he were addressing not just those in the room, but also future generations. He boldly assumed that his words would matter.

Application

- **Use passion to anchor memory:** Henry's words survive not because they were eloquent, but because they conveyed an emotional truth. Deliver your speech with energy and conviction, aiming to make the audience feel as well as think.

- **Engage the senses:** Use vivid imagery to paint a mental picture. Henry's reference to "chains" and "slavery" contrasted starkly with the freedom he envisioned, creating an indelible emotional impression. His audience could picture what the stakes looked like.

- **In practice:** Before crafting your next speech, consider what the most quotable takeaway will be. Build toward it with deliberate pacing, repetition, and imagery.

Exercise

Take an important message from your work or life. Rewrite it with a vivid metaphor or image. Then practice delivering it with dramatic pacing and pauses.

Personal Connection: The Impact Of Words

I was nine years old when I first heard Patrick Henry's speech. The power of his words ignited something in me. This speech, more than any other, made me want to become an effective speaker. I thought, "Someday, I hope my words can leave a fraction of the impact it had on me." I'm still striving toward that goal.

One of the bravest people I've ever met is Fengsuo Zhou. Back in June 1989, as a twenty-one-year-old student, he was one of many protesters who stood several yards away from the Chinese Communist Party's tanks at Tiananmen Square in Beijing. Fengsuo once told me, "I translated the US Constitution and Declaration of Independence into Mandarin and read it to other students. Sadly, many of those students were killed."[17]

On June 4, 2024, in recognition of the thirty-fifth anniversary of the Tiananmen Square massacre, Fengsuo and two current Chinese-born students spoke at a US congressional hearing. I coached them on how to share their stories with more drama, such as holding up bloody towels or medals awarded to Chinese soldiers for shooting fellow citizens. It was amazing to watch them speak confidently and persuasively, while reliving the injustice they experienced.

During my research of that event, which the Chinese Communist Party has tried to erase from history, I visited the June 4th Memorial Museum, a New York City museum dedicated to those who lost their lives at Tiananmen. I also watched a CNN documentary about the event, which showed an image of a sign that had the words "Give me liberty, or give me death" in both English and Mandarin.[18] More than two hundred years after those words were first spoken, they are still inspiring leaders all over the world who suffocate under tyranny.

A brave Chinese student, whom we will call "Koala," attended my speaking coaching program and shared her story of being imprisoned for one year due to her activism as a legal assistant to a human rights lawyer in China. She said, "Humiliation and mental torture were a constant theme."[19] During her 364 days of captivity, she never saw the sun. After being nominally released on bail, she was transferred to another location where she had the chance to see her parents.

One evening, on her way back to the hotel where she and her parents were staying under police surveillance, her accompanying guards lost sight of her. Koala seized the opportunity to escape, hiding in a convenience store and then wandering the streets for three hours. She knew she would eventually be caught and punished, but for those three hours, she relished the freedom that had been denied to her.

After Koala shared this story with our group, she became confident enough to repeat it in front of audiences in New York City and San Francisco. This is what having the courage and confidence to speak out entails.

Every year on July 4, I lead a reading of the Declaration of Independence. On July 4, 2024, as I was coaching leaders of the nongovernmental organization Human Rights in China, we went around the room with the leaders each reading one paragraph at a time. Later, we discussed the ideals of the document. It was a reminder of the enduring power of words to inspire and generate the change required to promote everyone's rights to life, liberty, and pursuit of happiness.

A Lesson For Liberty's Leaders: The Power Of Courageous Speech

Patrick Henry's iconic "Give Me Liberty, or Give Me Death" speech transcends time, offering a blueprint for conquering fears and galvanizing others to action. Analyzing his speech can help you confront the fear of public speaking, the fear of speaking freely, and the fear of being forgotten. The lasting power of his example demonstrates the enduring relevance of courageous communication for leaders.

Henry's speech was both a call for revolution and a brilliant exercise in ethos, logos, and pathos. By speaking with moral authority, he established his character (ethos), aligning his message with enduring principles of liberty and justice. His meticulous preparation ensured that his arguments (logos) were clear, logical, and impossible to ignore. And finally, through his use of emotionally charged language, vivid imagery, and dramatic delivery, Henry's ability to rouse sentiment (pathos) captured the hearts of his audience.

Your voice is your power. Use it wisely, boldly, and with purpose. As Henry's speech shows, the courage to speak not only transforms moments but also shapes history.

We next turn to Abraham Lincoln, who carried forward the tradition of courageous speech. His ability to deliver clear messages with moral conviction would unite a nation in crisis.

CHAPTER 4

Conceived In Liberty

I believe that I will never be old enough to speak without embarrassment when I have (nothing) to talk about.

ABRAHAM LINCOLN[1]

Let's fast-forward from 1775 to 1863 as we continue studying great speakers. Slavery—brutal, dehumanizing, and long accepted as a fact of life—had existed in nearly every major civilization, from ancient Egypt and Greece to Rome and medieval Europe. But beyond being immoral, slavery was deeply impractical. It stifled innovation, crushed initiative, and created a system where productivity had to be forced rather than earned. People working under coercion don't create; they survive. And, societies built on forced labor eventually rot from within.

In their book, *It's Getting Better All the Time*, authors Stephen Moore and Julian L. Simon display a chart that shows how historically up to 90 percent of humans were either slaves or serfs.[2] It wasn't until the Enlightenment, with its emphasis on individualism, reason, and self-government, that slavery and serfdom were fundamentally challenged and eventually ended by English-speaking nations.

Although the United States was consciously conceived in liberty, this promise was not extended to all. The American founders and framers, despite their ideals, were not prepared to resolve the contradiction of slavery. Instead, they took tentative steps, such as banning the importation of enslaved people in 1808. However, the American South continued this brutal practice, leading to a higher likelihood of conflict with the North as the nation expanded westward. The question loomed: Could a divided house endure? Would the industrial, capitalist, free North prevail over the feudal, agrarian, slaveholding South?

No country had ever fought a civil war over the issue of slavery. When Abraham Lincoln ran for president, his aim was to preserve the Union. But after his election, southern states seceded, leading to the outbreak of the US Civil War at Fort Sumter in April 1861. Two years later, both sides were still entrenched in conflict. In July 1863, the Battle of Gettysburg in Pennsylvania became the bloodiest scene of the war, costing fifty-one thousand casualties.

The Gettysburg Address

In the months after this battle, Pennsylvania Judge David Wills organized a dedication ceremony for the fallen soldiers. He invited Edward Everett, one of the most acclaimed speakers of the era, to deliver the keynote presentation. Despite being ill, Abraham Lincoln was also invited to say a few words.

While Everett spoke for two hours, it was Lincoln's brief, though targeted, remarks that would echo through history, emphasizing the principles upon which the United States was founded.[3] Given its brevity, I include in full the text of the Gettysburg Address:

FOURSCORE and seven years ago our fathers brought forth on this continent a new nation, conceived in liberty and dedicated to the proposition that all men are created equal. Now we are engaged in a great civil war, testing whether that nation, or any nation, so conceived and so dedicated, can long endure. We are met on a great battlefield of that war. We have come to dedicate a portion of that field as a final resting place for those who here gave their lives that that nation might live. It is altogether fitting and proper that we should do this. But, in a larger sense, we cannot dedicate—we cannot consecrate—we cannot hallow—this ground. The brave men, living and dead, who struggled here have consecrated it far above our poor power to add or to detract. The world will little note nor long remember what we say here, but it can never forget what they did here. It is for us, the living, rather to be dedicated here to the unfinished work which they who fought here have thus far so nobly advanced. It is rather for us to be here dedicated to the great task remaining before us—that from these honored dead we take increased devotion to that cause for which they gave the last full measure of devotion; that we here highly resolve that these dead shall not have died in vain; that this nation, under God, shall have a new birth of freedom; and that government of the people, by the people, for the people, shall not perish from the earth.[4]

Let us unpack Lincoln's Gettysburg Address from the perspective of Aristotle's principles of ethos, logos, and pathos.

Ethos: Moral Authority And Leadership

Abraham Lincoln's ethos in the Gettysburg Address is rooted in his moral authority, his integrity, and his commitment to the principle of equality before the law—a principle so fundamental that he framed it as the cause worth fighting and dying for. Lincoln's opening lines immediately establish his credibility by tying his presidency to the founding ideals of the United States: "FOURSCORE and seven years ago our fathers brought forth on this continent a new nation, conceived in liberty and dedicated to the proposition that all men are created equal."

By invoking the Declaration of Independence, Lincoln anchors his authority in America's founding principles. He is not asserting his personal power but reinforcing that his leadership is dedicated to the nation's highest ideals. This demonstrates integrity because he is aligning his role as President with this worthy cause.

Lincoln further builds his ethos by acknowledging that the true consecration of Gettysburg did not come from his words, but from the soldiers who fought there: "The brave men, living and dead, who struggled here have consecrated it far above our poor power to add or detract." By showing deference to those who lost their lives, Lincoln presents himself as a leader who serves the cause rather than a commander demanding obedience. This tone makes his moral authority more compelling as he's not glorifying war but honoring human loss.

Lincoln's entire speech builds toward one defining moral argument: The Union must be preserved because it is fighting for the principle of equality before the law. He makes this clear when he calls on the living to continue the unfinished work of the fallen: "It is for us, the living, rather, to be dedicated here to the unfinished work which they who fought here have thus far so nobly advanced." This "unfinished work" is not just a military victory; it is the survival of a nation based on equality and liberty. For Lincoln, integrity meant preserving the Union as a political entity and as a moral project that upholds the idea that all men are created equal.

In the final call to action, Lincoln delivers his most powerful ethical charge: "that government of the people, by the people, and for the people, shall not perish from the earth." This is the moral stake of the war: If the Union loses, it is not just a loss of land or power, but a betrayal of the very idea of self-government and individual rights. Lincoln's ethos is strongest here because he is not simply asking people to fight for territory; he is asking them to fight for a world in which the rule of law protects the rights of every individual.

Lincoln was not what Thomas Paine deridingly referred to as a "sunshine patriot."[5] His leadership was guided by conviction, not political expediency. His commitment to equality and self-government was not negotiable, even when facing fierce opposition. In this speech, his moral credibility rests on his dedication to principles that transcend one man's presidency. Through historic grounding and unwavering moral commitment, Lincoln solidifies himself as a leader of profound integrity who sees himself as carrying the torch of liberty. This is what makes his ethos so compelling and enduring.

Logos: Integrating America's Founding With Its Long-Term Survival

Lincoln presents a tight, logical progression that frames the Civil War as an existential test of America's founding ideals. His reasoning follows a five-step chain of logic, compelling his audience to see the necessity of continuing to fight for liberty:

1. Defining the core principles of liberty and equality as the nation's foundation: Lincoln begins with a historical premise: "FOURSCORE and seven years ago our fathers brought forth on this continent, a new nation, conceived in liberty and dedicated to the proposition that all men are created equal." He frames equality not as an abstract idea but as the defining feature of American identity, meaning any threat to equality threatens liberty and the nation's survival.

2. The war as a test of survival: Lincoln logically transitions from principle to predicament: "Now we are engaged in a great civil war, testing whether that nation, or any nation, so conceived and so dedicated, can long endure." This is a pivotal shift as he positions

the Civil War not as a regional conflict, but as a test of whether a nation founded on equality and liberty can last. The implied question is, if a nation based on liberty cannot withstand internal division, what does it say about the viability of the constitutional republic itself?

3. The loss of life as proof of the principle's importance: Lincoln argues that the fallen soldiers have already validated the significance of this cause through their actions: "The brave men, living and dead, who struggled here have consecrated it far above our poor power to add or detract." This is a logical consequence: if men are willing to die for a cause, it proves that the cause holds real-world significance, not just theoretical value. Lincoln's logic: if people have given their lives for liberty, the living must ensure those deaths were not in vain.

4. The responsibility of the living to continue the struggle: Lincoln then shifts the focus to those who are still alive: "It is for us, the living, rather to be dedicated here to the unfinished work which they who fought here have thus far so nobly advanced." His reasoning follows naturally: If the war is a test of America's founding ideals, and the soldiers have given their lives for those ideals, then the living must continue to work. He presents continuing the fight as the only rational response. To do otherwise would mean abandoning the cause for which so many have already died.

5. The conclusion: self-government must endure: Lincoln's closing statement cements the logical progression: "and that government of the people, by the people, for the people, shall not perish from the earth." This is the ultimate point of his argument. If equality is the nation's foundation, and the war is a test of its endurance, and the soldiers have given their lives for it, then the only logical path is to ensure that government of the people survives. Lincoln moves

from historical precedent to present struggle to future mandate, forcing his audience to recognize that the survival of the republic itself depends on their actions.

Pathos: Aspiration In Mourning

Lincoln's famous speech is steeped in emotion, laced with reverence, gratitude, and resolve. He speaks not just as a president but as a mourner, standing before a grieving nation. His words channel sorrow into commitment, turning the pain of loss into a rallying cry for perseverance. He honors the fallen with a solemn recognition of their loss, stating they had given "the last full measure of devotion." These words are deeply personal, evoking an image of men who gave everything, down to their final breath, for the cause of freedom. For Lincoln's audience, many of whom lost brothers, sons, and fathers in the war, this phrase would resonate profoundly. By framing their deaths as a complete act of devotion, Lincoln elevates their cost beyond personal loss, transforming it into an act of nobility.

He reinforces the nobility of their action by declaring, "we cannot dedicate—we cannot consecrate—we cannot hallow—this ground." With this statement, Lincoln shifts the focus away from himself and the ceremony, acknowledging that no speech, no matter how eloquent, could truly consecrate the battlefield more than the soldiers' blood already had. This could have struck a profound chord with his listeners, many of whom stood in mourning of loved ones who had died just months before. By voicing this shared grief, Lincoln builds an emotional bridge between himself and his audience.

Lincoln calls for gratitude by acknowledging deeds over words: "The world will little note nor long remember what we say here, but it can never forget what they did here." This statement is both deeply modest and strikingly powerful. By downplaying his own speech, he directs all attention to the courage of the fallen. The emotional impact of these words is profound. For a grieving family, it is a reassurance that their loved ones did not die in vain. For soldiers still fighting, it is a reminder that their struggle will be remembered long after the war is over. Lincoln's call to action is that if speeches do not define history, deeds do. The weight of responsibility shifts onto the audience. What will they do to ensure these men did not die for nothing?

But Lincoln does not leave his audience in sorrow; he lifts them with a vision of renewal. He urges "that this nation, under God, shall have a new birth of freedom." The phrase "new birth of freedom" evokes a powerful image: Out of death and destruction, something new can arise. The Civil War was not just a tragedy; it was a transformation.

This emotional appeal offers a sense of redemption to those who have suffered, implying that through their actions, a freer and more just nation can emerge. This was not just abstract hope. Lincoln spoke to men who had lost everything and needed to believe that their losses meant something. This phrase would have filled them with purpose, giving them the emotional strength to persevere.

He concludes with a mission: "that government of the people, by the people, for the people, shall not perish from the earth." These final words are not a promise but a challenge. The implication is clear: If the Union fails, the republic could disappear from the world forever.

For Lincoln's audience, this sobering thought stirred their emotions. He makes them feel responsible for the survival of liberty itself. This responsibility transcends personal loss, political division, and even the war itself. This is the power of pathos at its finest.

Overcoming Common Fears

Abraham Lincoln's speeches, particularly the Gettysburg Address, offer enduring lessons for addressing common fears such as public embarrassment, criticism, and heckling. By examining Lincoln's responses to these challenges, we can extract actionable strategies to conquer these fears in our own speaking and leadership endeavors.

Fear Of Public Embarrassment

Lesson: Abraham Lincoln, during the famous 1858 debates with Stephen Douglas (where each debater would speak for up to two uninterrupted hours at a time), faced ridicule for his unpolished style, unconventional appearance, and, notably, his high-pitched voice. Observers described his voice as "shrill, squeaking, piping, unpleasant" and "high-keyed."[6]

Instead of letting this undermine him, he used various techniques to connect with his audience, even when facing embarrassment. For instance, Lincoln's clear diction allowed his words to resonate with listeners, even in large outdoor settings. His precise articulation ensured that his message was understood, regardless of vocal pitch. This clarity helped his voice carry over crowds, making his speech impactful despite initial perceptions.

Lincoln focused on the substance of his speeches, believing that a compelling message would overshadow delivery flaws. By concentrating on well-structured arguments and relatable anecdotes, he engaged audiences effectively. This approach demonstrated that the power of ideas could transcend vocal limitations.

Regarding how his appearance was overshadowed, during Lincoln's 1860 Cooper Union address in New York, a literary critic had this to say: "When Lincoln rose to speak, I was greatly disappointed. He was tall, tall—oh, how tall! and so angular and awkward that I had, for an instant, a feeling of pity for so ungainly a man . . . . But pretty soon he began to get into his subject; he straightened up, made regular and graceful gestures; his face lighted as with an inward fire; the whole man was transfigured. I forgot his clothes, his personal appearance, and his individual peculiarities. Presently, forgetting myself, I was on my feet with the rest, yelling like a wild Indian, cheering this wonderful man."[7] The ability to change an audience's preconceived notions was one of Lincoln's hallmarks as a speaker.

Application

- **Embrace imperfections:** Use clear diction and articulation to turn perceived weaknesses into moments of relatability.

- **Focus on strengths:** Highlight the aspects of your delivery—content clarity, logical flow, or storytelling—that connect most with your audience.

- **Build resilience:** Prepare for potential mockery by practicing responses that reflect confidence and grace.

Exercise

Write down one personal trait or characteristic you fear might be adversely judged during a presentation. Craft a clear and eloquent response that you could use to defuse tension. Practice delivering it confidently in front of a trusted friend or mentor.

Fear Of Being Criticized

Lesson: Throughout his presidency, Lincoln faced intense criticism from both his supporters and opponents. In *The Life and Times of Frederick Douglass*, the author initially criticized Lincoln for being too slow in addressing slavery: "Mr. Lincoln seemed tardy, cold, dull, and indifferent . . ."[8] The *Brooklyn Eagle* stated that Lincoln merited "the deepest disgrace that the crushing indignation of a whole people can inflict." Also, the *New York Tribune* forecast morbidly, "Mr. Lincoln may live a hundred years without having so good a chance to die."[9]

In a famous 1862 letter to Horace Greeley, he clarified his position on slavery in a way that acknowledged public criticism while staying true to his principles. His response to criticism—whether to his presidency in general or the Emancipation Proclamation—was not to dismiss or ignore it but to engage with it directly, demonstrating resolve: "My paramount object in this struggle *is* to save the Union, and is *not* either to save or to destroy slavery. If I could save the Union without freeing *any* slave I would do it, and if I could save it by freeing *all* the slaves I would do it."[10]

This letter acknowledges the criticisms from both sides. Abolitionists believed Lincoln was not doing enough, while proslavery factions and Unionists feared he was going too far. His response shows that he was fully aware of the competing pressures but remained committed to his larger strategic goal: preserving the Union.

Yet, Lincoln's actions demonstrate that he did not compromise his deep moral conviction. While he framed the Emancipation Proclamation as a wartime necessity, it was also a fulfillment of his long-held opposition to slavery, where he considered it a *moral wrong*, even if he initially prioritized preserving the Union.

Lincoln understood that great leaders inevitably face criticism. His unwavering commitment to principles, even when attacked by both allies and opponents, demonstrates that true leadership requires resilience. His ability to maintain focus amidst harsh criticism makes him an enduring model of courage and conviction.

┌─ **Application** ─────────────────────────────────

- **Anticipate criticism:** Expect criticism, especially when presenting bold ideas. Prepare responses rooted in your values and evidence.

- **Stay grounded in purpose:** Use your core mission as a compass to navigate and address criticism without losing focus.

- **Learn and improve:** Criticism can be constructive. View valid critiques as opportunities to refine your message or delivery. You might even need to change your mind about something if someone presents well-founded counterevidence. Doing so could enhance your credibility by earning respect from your audience for your commitment to truth-seeking.

└──

Exercise

After your next presentation, invite feedback from a trusted colleague or audience member. Ask: "What resonated with you?" "What could I improve?" Reflect on how you can integrate this feedback without compromising your core message.

Fear Of Being Heckled And Losing Focus

Lesson: During the Lincoln-Douglas debates, Lincoln faced significant challenges, including heckling from the audience and intense opposition from Stephen Douglas's supporters. Despite the adversarial environment, Lincoln maintained his composure and focused on countering his opponent's points. His ability to stay on point despite heckling demonstrated his strength as an orator and potential leader.

---Application---

- **Practice under pressure:** Rehearse your speech in a noisy environment or in front of a mock audience instructed to interrupt or distract you. This will prepare you for real-world disruptions.

- **Use humor strategically:** Respond to hecklers with lighthearted, nonconfrontational remarks to defuse tension while maintaining focus.

- **Stay anchored in your message:** Remember your key points, ensuring that interruptions don't derail your delivery.

Exercise

Practice delivering a five-minute speech to a group of friends who act as hecklers. Focus on maintaining composure and redirecting interruptions back to your message. Afterward, debrief with the group to evaluate your responses.

Lincoln's ability to overcome fears of public embarrassment, criticism, and heckling reminds us that these challenges are not barriers but opportunities to connect more deeply with our audience. His grace, authenticity, and moral conviction continue to serve as a guide for speakers and leaders alike. By applying these lessons and practicing with intentionality, you, too, can rise above your fears and deliver messages that inspire and endure.

Additional Masterful Elements Of Lincoln

Power of pause: Lincoln's mastery of pacing and the use of pauses helped his words land with even greater power. He delivered each line of the Gettysburg Address slowly and with intention, allowing the audience time to absorb each phrase and reflect on its meaning. His pauses were not just silences. They were moments for his audience to internalize his words, giving weight to every sentence. This technique was particularly impactful given the brevity of the speech.

Lincoln understood that the pause was as much a rhetorical tool as the words themselves. Pauses allow listeners to reflect, process, and emotionally engage with what's being said. Lincoln's pauses allowed for solemn reflection on the lives lost on the Gettysburg battlefield, infusing phrases such as "we cannot dedicate—we cannot consecrate—we cannot hallow—this ground" with a reverence fitting the occasion.

Simplicity: Lincoln's language was simple yet profound. He avoided grandiose phrases and complex vocabulary, choosing instead words that were universally understood and accessible to everyone. He knew that his audience included people of all educational backgrounds. By choosing simple, clear language, he made a choice to reach as many people as possible and not make anyone feel excluded.

For example, Lincoln's opening line, "FOURSCORE and seven years ago," may seem poetic to us today. Yet, it was a straightforward way to reference a specific point in history (1776) that held deep significance for his audience. Lincoln ensured that his message of national unity would not be lost on anyone present, allowing the ideas of liberty and equality to reach every ear, heart, and mind in the audience.

As a Gettysburg contrast, Edward Everett, the keynote speaker, was a renowned orator who spoke for two hours, delivering an elaborate speech filled with complex sentence structures and classical allusions. For instance, contrast Lincoln's opening line (above) with Everett's: "Standing beneath this serene sky, overlooking these broad fields now reposing from labors of the waning year, the mighty Alleghenies dimly towering before us, the graves of our brethren beneath our feet . . ."[11]

Lincoln's simplicity also lent an immortal quality to his speech. Because his words were easy to grasp, they became memorable and have endured in the American consciousness for generations. Lincoln's commitment to simplicity was not a compromise but a strength, as it allowed his words to strike a chord that we still hear today.

Evocative imagery: This is one of the most striking elements of Lincoln's speech. Through his choice of words, Lincoln painted powerful mental pictures that stirred his audience's emotions and encouraged them to consider the broader implications of the Civil War while honoring the lives lost. For example, the phrase "a new birth of freedom" suggests the idea of renewal, implying that the United States could emerge from the horrors of war as a stronger, more unified nation committed more fully to its founding principles.

Meanwhile, "the last full measure of devotion" evokes the ultimate cost of the soldiers who died at Gettysburg. This line reminds the living of the great price of war and the obligation to honor those who gave everything for the nation's ideals.

By using such vivid imagery, Lincoln not only conveyed his message effectively but also left a lasting emotional impression. The imagery invited listeners to reflect on the meaning of freedom and unity, reinforcing his call for national dedication to the principles of America's constitutional republic.

Personal Connection: Honest Abe Still Inspires

Reflecting on Lincoln's legacy, I recall my childhood admiration for him. Often, I gazed at a five-dollar bill (or a copper penny when I was really young) and thanked him for preserving the Union and ending slavery.

Many years later, when my dearest, Carrie-Ann Biondi, and I visited Gettysburg, our usual smiles disappeared from our faces. The solemn atmosphere, marked by the countless lives lost, brought the significance of Lincoln's words into sharp focus. The memorials erected in Gettysburg, some bearing the text of the Gettysburg Address, are reminders of the great cost those soldiers made in the name of freedom. They invite us to continue the hard work of maintaining liberty.

However, during one of my recent group coaching calls, I had Carrie-Ann read the opening of Lincoln's address the way a sixth-grade honors student would do it. She memorized the words, channeled her inner twelve-year-old, and recited them quickly and evenly. When she finished, the group heard loud laughter from my brother Peter, who said, "Ouch! Those words are eternal. You can't go by that fast, without any emphasis!" I was hoping to evoke such a reaction by having Carrie-Ann give a poor delivery of this famous speech.

Next, I had Peter read the words, which he did as an experienced preacher would. He used a sonorous tone, pausing for emphasis on particular words, and finished with a flourish. Clearly, Lincoln's words and message still mean something, as Peter's passionate delivery of this timeless speech shows. Lincoln would have been proud.

The fight for liberty isn't just a relic of history—it's an ongoing struggle that demands courage and unwavering moral conviction. One of my most heroic coaching clients, José Mora, turned down a blackmail payment by Venezuela's dictatorship run by government thugs. He was beaten, tortured, and scheduled to be executed. Fortunately, he escaped the day before the scheduled execution and made his way to the US, where he now embodies the American dream. I help him tell his story to people all over the world. Frankly, I'm so proud of him I usually end up telling his story more than he does. When I asked, "José, why did you turn down $1.5 million in bribes?" he replied, "Many people took the money, but I knew it was wrong and must live up to my name and be moral." Well done, José Mora!

Lessons For Liberty's Leaders: The Enduring Impact Of Courageous Speech

Abraham Lincoln's Gettysburg Address transcends its historical context. Its brilliance lies in its brevity, universal appeal, and moral conviction. At just 268 words, Lincoln demonstrated that powerful communication doesn't require length but clarity. He distilled the essence of liberty, equality, and justice into a few unforgettable phrases, creating a message that resonates across generations.

What makes Lincoln's speech timeless?

- **Brevity with impact:** Lincoln's concise delivery ensured that every word mattered, leaving no room for filler or fluff.

- **Universal values:** By invoking the principle of equality and the quest for freedom, Lincoln addressed ideas that transcend time and culture. Nearly everyone wants equal treatment and to live life on their own terms.

- **Moral conviction:** Delivered at a moment of profound national crisis, Lincoln's words reminded his audience of the enduring struggle to live up to America's founding ideals.

For leaders, Lincoln's speech offers this essential lesson: clarity, purpose, and courage transform fleeting words into enduring legacies.

The Gettysburg Address reminds us that even in the face of division and despair, a well-crafted message can unite and inspire action.

As we reflect on Lincoln's example, we now turn to another towering figure who spoke with conviction and lived by the principles of self-reliance and moral courage: Frederick Douglass.

Lincoln and Douglass knew and respected each other. They understood that words are a tool for both personal and social transformation. In the next chapter, we'll explore how Douglass's life as a self-made man offers a road map for overcoming adversity, speaking the truth, and creating lasting change.

CHAPTER 5

Becoming Self-Made

To suppress free speech is a double wrong.
It violates the rights of the hearer as well as those of the speaker.
It is just as criminal to rob a man of his right to speak and hear
as it would be to rob him of his money.

FREDERICK DOUGLASS[1]

I n 1840s America, as the movement toward abolition of slavery took hold, Frederick Douglass, newly escaped from enslavement, settled in New England and came to meet the leading abolitionist, William Lloyd Garrison, editor of *The Liberator.*

The two initially bonded as Garrison set up Douglass to speak and write about the brutality he endured under enslavement and how his life had changed. The first time Garrison heard Douglass speak, he proclaimed, "I rose, and declared that PATRICK HENRY, of revolutionary fame, never made a speech more eloquent in the cause of liberty, than the one we just listened to from the lips of that haunted fugitive."[2] That was a good start, but eventually Douglass felt his voice was being limited and wanted to strike out on his own.

Let's step back to see how Douglass got to this point. He was born into enslavement, denied education, and told that his life belonged to others. A system designed to keep him dependent and powerless deliberately suppressed his humanity, intellect, and potential.

As a child, Douglass had no formal education. It was illegal for enslaved people to learn to read and write, but he saw the value of both. He said: "Though conscious of the difficulty of learning without a teacher, I set out with high hope, and a fixed purpose, at whatever cost of trouble, to learn how to read."[3]

Douglass refused to wait for freedom or education to be handed to him. He took action. He taught himself to read and write through relentless effort and ingenuity. He befriended local white children and used clever strategies, such as offering them bread in exchange for lessons. He secretly studied newspapers and other materials, building his literacy bit by bit. Literacy became his gateway to understanding the world around him and plotting his escape to freedom.

His defining philosophy was simple and can be encapsulated in an apocryphal expression attributed to Douglass: "I prayed for twenty years for my freedom but received no answer until I prayed with my legs." His transformation began the moment he chose action over passivity.

His courage and determination culminated in a daring escape. Disguised as a sailor, carrying forged documents, he boarded a train from Baltimore to New York. His ability to read, plan, and execute his escape was not just a testament to his intellect; it was a triumph of self-reliance.

Douglass's first jobs as a free man were life-changing. He said: "I was now my own master. It was a happy moment, the rapture of which can be understood only by those who have been slaves. It was the first work, the reward of which was to be entirely my own."[4] Now, all the money he earned was his. It was a moment of profound personal pride. He became unbound and seized control of his destiny. His work, his intellect, and his achievements were finally his own.

Douglass turned his industriousness into a life of intellectual and entrepreneurial success. He became a celebrated orator, an abolitionist leader, and the publisher of *The North Star*, a newspaper dedicated to advancing liberty and justice. He believed that the US Constitution was a sacred liberty document that recognized the potential for prosperity that freedom and hard work could create. His life was a living testament to his belief in self-reliance: "The man who will get up will be helped up; and the man who will not get up will be allowed to stay down," he said.[5]

After the US Civil War, Frederick Douglass became known as a powerful advocate of self-reliance. Douglass's "Self-Made Men"[6] speech, which he refined over the course of his life, underscores the principle that success is rooted in diligent effort and personal responsibility. Douglass firmly believed that reliance on hard work was the cornerstone of achieving greatness. Furthermore, he passionately advocated *self-dependence*, emphasizing that the freedom to strive and overcome rather than being bound by handouts was essential to individual dignity and social progress.

My analysis of Douglass's "Self-Made Men" speech using Aristotle's rhetorical principles—ethos, logos, and pathos—focuses on his key themes of work as the foundation of success and the value of self-dependence.

Ethos: Character And Credibility

Douglass's authority as a speaker and thinker is rooted in his life experience and philosophical insights. His ethos is built on a life that exemplifies the very ideals he advocates.

In his definition of self-made men, Douglass outlines the essence of character, resilience, and self-reliance: "By the term 'self-made men,' I mean especially what, to the popular mind, the term least imports . . . .

Self-made men are the men who, under peculiar difficulties and without the ordinary help of favoring circumstances, have attained knowledge, usefulness, power, and position."[7]

This definition anchors his credibility by tying the concept of self-made men directly to his own life story. As a man who escaped enslavement, educated himself, and rose to national prominence, Douglass personifies the qualities of perseverance and determination. His authority comes not from abstract theory, but from personal triumph over adversity. Although he doesn't say so explicitly, the idea of being "self-made" applies as much to women as to men.

Douglass goes further to illustrate the individual responsibility that defines self-made men: "If they have traveled far, they have made the road on which they have traveled. If they have ascended high, they have built their own ladder."[8]

This statement reinforces his moral authority by reflecting his self-reliant philosophy. He speaks with authenticity as someone who has personally "built his own ladder" to success, appealing to the respect of his audience for his life's example. It is not merely his words, but also the weight of his journey, that commands attention.

Douglass deepens his credibility and positions himself as both a philosopher and a practitioner of self-made principles by framing human potential as the ultimate subject of contemplation: "Man himself, with eyes turned inward upon his own wondrous attributes and powers, surpasses them all."[9] This profound observation demonstrates Douglass's understanding of human nature and the central role of introspection in shaping the moral, intellectual, and personal achievements that shape a society.

He also expands on the intellectual and moral heights to which humanity can aspire: "To human thought and inquiry he is broader than all visible worlds, loftier than all heights and deeper than all depths."[10]

Here, his reflections align him with the intellectual giants of history, adding depth and weight to his message. By intertwining his personal triumphs with a reverence for human potential, Douglass offers a vision of self-reliance that is both aspirational and achievable.

Douglass's ethos transcends his words; it is embodied in his life. His audience sees not only a man who overcame unimaginable odds, but also a thinker who elevates the human spirit to its rightful place of honor.

Douglass's life story is a testament to the power of self-reliance and the pursuit of knowledge, inspiring his audience to embrace their own potential. In his words and actions, Douglass calls on us to reflect on our own capabilities: Are we building our own ladders? Are we turning inward to recognize the limitless attributes of humanity? His life challenges us to rise, and in doing so, our society will also rise.

Logos: Rational Argument For Work, Freedom, And Knowledge

Douglass's "Self-Made Men" speech is a clinic in logos. He appeals to the rational mind by grounding his argument in cause and effect, a fundamental principle of logical reasoning. He does not rely on emotional pleas or abstract ideals alone; instead, he presents an empirical case for self-made success. His argument is structured around work, freedom, and knowledge as the essential ingredients for personal and social advancement.

Douglass makes a clear, rational assertion: success is tied directly to work. His repetition of the word "work" emphasizes the need for sustained effort, reinforcing the logical principle that input determines output. By stating that "allowing only ordinary ability and opportunity, we may explain success mainly by one word, and that word is WORK! WORK!! WORK!!! WORK!!!!"[11] he presents an unavoidable conclusion: Consistent effort leads to personal achievement. This logical structure leaves little room for counterarguments.

Douglass further clarifies this principle by rejecting the idea of waiting for external support or luck: "Certainly no one must wait for some kind of friend to put a springing board under his feet, upon which he may easily bound from the first round of the ladder onward and upward to its highest round."[12]

Here, Douglass dismisses dependency on external circumstances as illogical. He reasons that self-initiative is not just the most reliable path to success, but often the only path. The logic is straightforward: Waiting for assistance is a gamble, while taking action is a guarantee of progress.

Douglass then moves on to the relationship between effort and opportunity: "The man who will get up will be helped up; and the man who will not get up will be allowed to stay down. This rule may appear somewhat harsh, but in its general application and operation it is wise, just and beneficent."[13]

This statement presents a simple cause-and-effect argument. Douglass asserts that effort invites opportunity, while passivity ensures stagnation. His logical framework appeals to justice: Individuals who take responsibility for their lives are rewarded, while those who refuse to act remain in their circumstances. The implicit reasoning is that society cannot function based on entitlement; self-reliance must precede external aid.

This argument is further grounded in the practicality of independence: "Personal independence is a virtue, and it is the soul out of which comes the sturdiest manhood. But there can be no independence without a large share of self-dependence, and this virtue cannot be bestowed. It must be developed from within."[14]

Through this statement, Douglass ties independence to the logical requirement of self-dependence. He systematically dismantles the idea that independence can be granted, instead illustrating that it must be cultivated through effort and internal strength.

Aristotle first called man "the rational animal," and Douglass elaborates on this: "Were I called upon to point out the broadest and most permanent distinction between mankind and other animals, it would be this: their earnest desire for the fullest knowledge of human nature on all its many sides."[15]

Douglass's reasoning is grounded in a logical comparison between humans and animals. He argues that intellectual curiosity and the desire for self-knowledge are unique to humanity. This distinction elevates the importance of studying human nature, as it is the foundation of all progress and understanding. Without the drive to explore and comprehend, humanity would be indistinguishable from other creatures.

Douglass's "Self-Made Men" speech builds a compelling logical framework that ties success, freedom, and knowledge to individual effort and intellectual curiosity. By systematically connecting work to success, effort to opportunity, and knowledge to progress, Douglass crafts an argument that is as inspiring as it is rational.

His logic challenges us to ask: Are we investing the effort necessary to achieve our goals? Are we cultivating self-reliance to secure independence? Are we valuing knowledge as the cornerstone of personal growth? Douglass's speech reminds us that reason and effort, when combined, have the power to transform lives and elevate humanity.

Pathos: Stirring Dignity, Hope, And Urgency

In "Self-Made Men," Douglass evokes a powerful sense of dignity and urgency by framing justice not as an abstract principle but as a moral imperative. Focusing on the plight of newly freed slaves, he appeals to the audience's shared humanity and conscience. Justice, he argues, must be made real in the present, not only acknowledged in the abstract. "The nearest approach to justice to the negro for the past is to do him justice in the present . . . . Give him all the facilities for honest and successful livelihood, and in all honorable avocations receive him as a man among men."[16]

Here, Douglass taps into the emotional weight of past injustice, not through anger, but through a plea for dignity. He does not ask for charity or pity; he demands opportunity. The emotional force of this passage compels his audience to recognize that the true path to reconciliation is action, not sentiment. By framing justice as immediate and necessary, he moves the audience to feel the weight of responsibility as justice delayed is justice denied.

Douglass also confronts human suffering and struggle head-on, evoking both hope and fear when he declares: "Nothing can bring to man so much of happiness or so much of misery as man himself. Today he exalts himself to heaven by his virtues and achievements; to-morrow he smites with sadness and pain, by his crimes and follies."[17]

This passage deeply resonates with the audience's emotions because it acknowledges universal human struggle—the battle between good and evil, virtue and vice. Douglass taps into the shared human fear of falling into moral or personal failure, while simultaneously offering hope that one's choices can elevate them. This emotional contrast sparks a sense of urgency in the audience: One must act now to pursue virtue and avoid self-destruction.

To further inspire, Douglass paints a vivid, awe-inspiring image of human potential: "It is the faith of the race that in man there exists far outlying continents of power, thought, and feeling, which remain to be discovered, explored, cultivated, made practical, and glorified."[18]

This metaphor of undiscovered continents awakens a sense of wonder and limitless possibility. By likening personal growth to uncharted lands waiting to be explored, Douglass stirs the imagination of his listeners, making them feel as though they, too, can embark on a heroic journey of self-discovery and achievement.

He then elevates human potential into a divine force: "From man comes all that we know or can imagine of heaven and earth, of time and eternity." This heroic vision of man's creative power evokes pride, ambition, and optimism. It is an emotional call to recognize that each person holds the power to shape the world, reinforcing self-belief and aspiration in their audience. Douglass makes each listener feel important, as if their individual contribution could reshape history.

Douglass's pathos succeeds because it does three things emotionally: It compels moral urgency as he makes the need for justice immediate and personal. It acknowledges suffering while offering hope, as Douglass understands hardship but inspires his audience to rise above it. And it elicits pride and aspiration. Douglass calls upon the greatness of every individual, making them capable of extraordinary achievements.

By combining a call to justice, a warning against failure, and a vision of boundless human potential, Douglass ensures that his audience not only listens but also feels, believes, and acts.

Overcoming Common Fears

Douglass's "Self-Made Men" speech offers valuable lessons for overcoming three common fears: stating the obvious and being ignored, being misunderstood, and not knowing enough about the topic.

Stating The Obvious And Being Ignored

Lesson: This fear often arises from the belief that your ideas lack novelty or originality, leading to the concern that your audience may dismiss you. Douglass tackled this fear by embracing and reinforcing fundamental truths. In his speech, he repeatedly stated, "Men are not made by circumstances, but by the use they make of them."

This simple but profound statement underscored his belief in personal responsibility and agency. Douglass understood that repetition of essential truths ensured they would resonate deeply and be remembered. He made the "obvious" compelling by tying it to vivid imagery, relatable anecdotes, and people's real-life struggles. By doing so, he transformed foundational truths into memorable insights.

Application

- To overcome this fear, embrace the idea that restating foundational truths is a service to your audience. Simple, clear ideas, when delivered with conviction and vividness, have the power to stick in the mind.

- Reframe the obvious as essential. Remember, what feels obvious to you may not be to your audience. Use memorable phrasing, rhetorical devices like repetition, and real-world examples to make your point impactful and relatable.

Exercise

Write down a simple truth or principle you believe in deeply, such as "Hard work pays off." Next, brainstorm three ways to illustrate this point using a personal story, a vivid metaphor or analogy, and a historical example (e.g., Douglass's perseverance). Rehearse delivering this idea with conviction, emphasizing clarity and emotional resonance.

Fear Of Being Misunderstood

Lesson: This fear stems from the possibility that your audience may misconstrue your message, leading to unintended consequences such as confusion, offense, or rejection. It can result in you either overcomplicating or hesitating to share your ideas.

Douglass often anticipated potential misunderstandings and addressed them directly. For example, because many people fatalistically accept the conditions that exist, he clarified the nature of the circumstances. In doing so, he made room for individual agency in "Self-Made Men": "Self-made men are the men who, under peculiar difficulties and without the ordinary help of favoring circumstances, have attained knowledge, usefulness, power, and position and have learned from themselves the best uses to which life can be put in this world . . . ."[19]

Douglass also understood that misinterpretation was a risk, especially when addressing controversial issues like slavery and individual responsibility. He countered this by crafting his arguments with precision and providing concrete examples to illustrate abstract concepts. Douglass demonstrated that clarity and directness can transform a potentially murky message into a powerful and persuasive one.

Application

Misunderstanding can be avoided by anticipating areas of confusion and addressing them proactively. You can simplify complex ideas without diluting their essence. Use clear, concise language to structure your speech logically. Also, address potential objections or ambiguities directly, using examples or analogies to reinforce your audience's understanding.

Exercise

Take a concept you want to communicate and explain it in three levels of detail: a one-sentence summary, a concise paragraph, and a detailed explanation with examples. Share these versions with a friend or mentor. Ask them for feedback, integrate it, and ask them to review the revised versions to ensure your ideas are clear and accessible at every level.

Fear Of Not Knowing Enough About The Topic

Lesson: This fear is rooted in self-doubt. Speakers worry they lack sufficient expertise or that their audience may question their credibility.

Douglass taught himself to read and write despite the significant barriers imposed by enslavement. This self-education gave him the knowledge and confidence to speak authoritatively. The Library of Congress has a painting of one of his famous expressions: "Once you learn to read, you will forever be free."[20] Douglass knew that knowledge is power. He didn't let gaps in formal education deter him. He committed to lifelong learning, which enabled him to speak on complex topics such as abolition, self-reliance, and the US Constitution with authority and depth.

Application

- Preparation is the antidote to self-doubt. Douglass's relentless pursuit of knowledge empowered him to speak with confidence, even in the face of skepticism. In fact, he was so articulate that audiences sometimes doubted that he was ever enslaved.

• One way to commit to thorough preparation is to research your topic deeply and organize your ideas to ensure clarity and coherence. Also, focus on continuous learning. Even if you feel unprepared in the moment, remind yourself that expertise is built over time, as Douglass's life demonstrates.

Exercise

Choose a specific topic you feel underprepared to speak about. Spend at least one hour researching it. Write down three key points you've learned and create a short outline for a speech or presentation. Practice delivering this outline to a trusted friend, focusing on clarity and confidence.

It is likely that you already know more about this topic than the audience you are addressing. Let their questions help you see gaps in your knowledge, so that you can do further research and keep integrating it into what you know.

Personal Connection: Landmarks Leaving Marks

When I was about eight years old, I took the subway with my mother from the Bronx to Harlem. When we climbed the stairs to the street, the first thing I saw was a grimy sign that read, "Frederick Douglass Boulevard." I thought, "What a manly name!" Tugging on my mother's arm, I asked, "Who's Frederick Douglass?" She stopped, looked up at the sign, and replied with a conviction I didn't fully understand at the time, "Frederick Douglass. There's no one like him."

That moment planted the seed of curiosity in my mind. Who was this man whose name carried such weight? My mother's words led me to dive into Douglass's life story. What I discovered profoundly shaped my own perspective on self-reliance, work, and courage.

Douglass As A Role Model For Leaders And Entrepreneurs

I often give walking tours in New York City, ending at the northwest corner of Central Park, where a statue of Douglass now stands. I share his story with participants, reminding them that Douglass's achievements benefit us all. His principles—self-reliance, courage, and dedication to justice—are timeless.

Douglass's story resonates deeply with anyone striving to create their own path, particularly entrepreneurs and leaders. His emphasis on the relationship between liberty and prosperity serves as a guiding principle for business leaders who understand the transformative power of freedom and responsibility.

One of my most memorable experiences as a speaker was sharing Douglass's letter to his former enslaver during a presentation. Instead of showing the words on a PowerPoint slide, as I've seen many speakers do, I pulled out an old envelope, opened it, and began reading a copy of the parchment paper letter aloud. The act was simple, but the words were powerful. One man in the audience, Jeffrey Baldwin, was visibly moved.

The Ripple Effect: Inspiring A New Generation

Like Douglass, Jeffrey understood the price of freedom. He had walked from Guatemala to the United States, seeking liberty. After my presentation, he mentioned how my speech had awakened something in him: "The mandates and curfews during COVID-19 reminded me of the curfews I endured as a kid in Guatemala." He said to his partner Levi, "I can't just sit by and watch this. I need to become more involved in the liberty movement."

Jeffrey joined the nonprofit LIBRE Initiative as a grassroots director and later became the director of the Initiative's parent organization, the LIBRE Institute. Watching him grow into a polished speaker and leader has been one of the most rewarding experiences of my career. He once said, "Robert, your speech changed my life. I knew I needed to work in the liberty movement." Like Douglass, Jeffrey embodies the power of self-reliance and the courage to act.

Douglass's life is more than a story of overcoming adversity. It is a road map for anyone striving to become self-made. His principles of work, independence, and moral conviction remind us that true freedom comes not from external aid but from within. His journey continues to inspire leaders, entrepreneurs, and citizens to rise above challenges, create their own opportunities, and contribute to a better society.

Douglass's message is clear: The path to freedom and success is paved with action, resilience, and self-reliance. His life proves that we are not defined by our circumstances, but by what we choose to do with them. And in that choice lies the power to inspire generations to come.

A Lesson For Liberty's Leaders

By embracing perseverance, dedication, and moral integrity, Douglass showed that anyone can achieve greatness, regardless of their starting point. His powerful use of ethos, logos, and pathos, combined with his commanding delivery, made his message hit home with his audience and continues to inspire generations. Douglass's example teaches us that through self-reliance, effort, and a commitment to ethical principles, we can rise above any challenge and shape our destinies.

As we move from the nineteenth to the twentieth century, we'll examine world leaders who wielded the power of speech to divide and oppress millions, as well as those who lifted their voices to unite and resist tyranny. From soaring rhetoric that united nations to dangerous demagoguery that led them astray, the century reveals a spectrum of how ideas shape history.

In the next chapter we will explore the enduring influence of Winston Churchill, who championed liberty, offering lessons for navigating the challenges of our modern world.

CHAPTER 6

Contrasting Tyrants
With A Leader

Of all the talents bestowed upon men, none is so precious as the gift
of oratory. He who enjoys it wields a power more durable than that
of a great king. He is an independent force in the world.

WINSTON CHURCHILL[1]

L eaving the nineteenth century and moving into the twentieth, a
new era dawned. Rapid advancements in technology caused the
relationship between ideas and action to intensify. The radio and
television, like Morse code and the printing press before them, expanded
the reach of ideas to mass audiences, but with greater speed and wider
impact.

These tools themselves, however, are neutral. They can be wielded to
uplift humanity or to tear it down. Think of the sage advice to Spider-
Man: "With great power there must also come—great responsibility."[2] The
twentieth century unfortunately witnessed the emergence of charismatic
speakers who harnessed the power of technology and the power of their
platform to default on that responsibility and further their destructive
ideologies. Among them, two figures stand out: Vladimir Lenin and
Adolf Hitler.

Pathos Without Ethos Or Logos

Lenin's oratory played a pivotal role in propelling one of history's deadliest ideologies: communism. This ideology, which caused tens of millions of deaths, was initially fueled by Lenin's potent speeches. His style of delivery was emotionally charged, crafted to stir up feelings of envy and class resentment. Visuals of Lenin often depict him on an improvised podium, arm outstretched, and face marked by intense conviction, as he passionately addressed the crowds.

His rhetoric was not aimed at reasoned debate or moral reflection; rather, it tapped into collective despair and anger, advocating violent revolution as the only solution. In his seminal 1917 text, *The State and Revolution*, he emphasizes this approach, stating repeatedly that overthrowing the bourgeois state via the proletarian state cannot occur without "violent revolution,"[3] a phrase he repeats eleven times. Such use of pathos, without ethos or logos, exemplifies how Lenin manipulated emotions to mobilize support for revolutionary action.

Hitler, another master manipulator of emotions, crafted his speeches with obsessive precision to inflame nationalistic fervor and advance the ugly agenda of National Socialism. Hitler understood the emotional power of spectacle, frequently staging his speeches in grand venues illuminated by imposing swastika banners and dramatic lighting. Every gesture, pause, and crescendo was rehearsed to heighten the emotional tension.

His speeches exploited deep-seated fears and prejudices, conjuring an imagined enemy to unify his audience in hatred. For example, in *Mein Kampf*, Hitler states, "in the big lie there is always a certain force of credibility; because the broad masses of a nation are always more easily corrupted in the deeper strata of their emotional nature than consciously or voluntarily."[4] What this means, in more plain language, is: "If you tell a big enough lie, it will be believed." Notably absent from Hitler's public presence is any evidence of quiet conversation or reasoned dialogue.

His rhetoric was tailored entirely for mass hysteria, with no space for individual reasoning or dissent.

Both Lenin and Hitler embodied the danger of unbridled pathos, that is, emotional appeal without the grounding of logic or moral integrity. In Aristotle's framework, their speeches were heavy on pathos, were empty of genuine logos, and twisted ethos to sell deceit as truth. The ethos they projected was a distorted one, built on dominance and the illusion of authority rather than ethical leadership. Their audiences, swept up in the emotional currents of anger, envy, and desperation, abandoned reason and moral reflection, leaving devastation in their wake.

The consequences were catastrophic. Lenin's oratory led to decades of repression under Soviet Communism, with gulags, purges, and engineered famines marking its legacy. Hitler's speeches, in turn, paved the way for the horrors of the Holocaust and global conflict of World War II. The emotional appeal that underpinned their rhetoric demonstrates the peril of persuasion disconnected from reason and ethical principles.

A Voice Of Reason Against Tyranny

In stark contrast to the manipulative and destructive rhetoric of Lenin and Hitler stood the unwavering voice of reason: Winston Churchill. By the late 1930s, Hitler's conquest of Europe seemed almost inevitable. The British government, led by Neville Chamberlain, pursued a policy of appeasement, most infamously embodied in the Munich Agreement of 1938, which allowed Nazi Germany to annex portions of Czechoslovakia. Chamberlain's declaration of securing "peace for our time" proved to be disastrously shortsighted, as Hitler continued his aggressive expansion.

Churchill, however, recognized the true nature of the Nazi threat early on and refused to compromise with tyranny. His warnings about Hitler's ambitions and the growing power of the Third Reich were ignored for years, relegating him to what he called his "wilderness years."[5] During this ten-year period (1929–1939), Churchill was without significant political power, yet he continued to speak out forcefully in Parliament and through his writings, warning of the dangers of appeasement and urging Britain to prepare for war. His steadfastness earned him criticism as a "warmonger," but history would vindicate his foresight.

Churchill's ability to anticipate the Nazi threat was rooted in his deep understanding of history, strategy, and the moral imperatives of leadership. He both studied and wrote history and saw value in the lessons it could teach us. This commitment to learning from the past allowed Churchill to see patterns others missed, which informed his belief that liberty and civilization could not coexist with the totalitarianism of Nazi Germany.

Churchill's moral courage and intellectual rigor stood in stark contrast to the propaganda-driven appeals of his adversaries, especially that of Hitler. While Hitler and Lenin used pathos to manipulate their audiences into blind allegiance, Churchill blended ethos, logos, and pathos to inspire rational action and moral resolve. When he finally became Prime Minister in 1940, speeches, such as "We Shall Fight on the Beaches," "Their Finest Hour," and "The Few," not only rallied the British people, but also galvanized the world to stand against tyranny.[6]

We Shall Fight On The Beaches

In June 1940, Europe was under the iron grip of Nazi Germany. France had surrendered and there are famous photos of Hitler smugly standing in front of the Eiffel Tower. On the brink of invasion, the United Kingdom stood alone. The British Expeditionary Force had just been evacuated from Dunkirk, leaving the nation vulnerable. It was in this moment of crisis that Winston Churchill, newly appointed prime minister, delivered his iconic "We Shall Fight on the Beaches" speech to the House of Commons. We'll see how Churchill used rhetorical principles to rally the British people to resist tyranny.

Ethos: Steadfast Leadership

Churchill's ethos—his credibility and character—was firmly established by his role as the prime minister during Britain's darkest hour. His leadership credentials were bolstered by his long history of warning against the Nazi threat, a position he held even when it was politically unpopular. His resilience is evident in his persistence to stand against a formidable enemy, preparing his nation for a long struggle, despite the odds.

He said: "I have myself full confidence that if all do their duty and if the best arrangements are made, as they are being made, we shall prove ourselves once again able to defend our island home, ride out the storms of war and outlive the menace of tyranny, if necessary, for years, if necessary, alone."[7]

This demonstrates his resilient spirit. His assurance that the nation's capability to withstand and overcome the dire situation underscores his role as a steadfast leader, showing a sense of hope and determination among the British people.

Churchill's ethos also came from his reputation for honesty and clarity. He didn't sugarcoat the situation, openly acknowledging the grave challenges ahead. His willingness to speak hard truths further solidified his credibility as a leader who could be trusted in a time of crisis.

By speaking not just as a statesman but as a fellow Briton, Churchill earned the trust of a nation in crisis. After the evacuation of Dunkirk, he candidly warned, "We must be very careful not to assign to this deliverance the attributes of a victory. Wars are not won by evacuations."[8] This moment revealed Churchill's ethos—his moral courage to tell the truth. He didn't try to spin a retreat into a triumph. Instead, he leveled with his people and, in doing so, built credibility that would carry them through the darkest days of war.

Logos: Structured Analysis Of Crisis And Rational Response

Churchill's speeches are renowned for their structured, logical approach. They clarify the stakes involved and outline Britain's defensive strategy during World War II. He adeptly begins by laying a foundation of stark realities, acknowledging the imminent threat while preparing the nation for potential outcomes.

He opens with a somber admission of the dire circumstances faced by the British Expeditionary Force: "I feared it would be my hard lot to announce the greatest military disaster in our long history."[9] This acknowledgment sets a serious tone that enhances the weight of his speech, ensuring that the gravity of the situation is clearly understood by his audience.

He continues by contrasting the capabilities and actions of the opposing forces. Describing the German military strategy, he notes: "The enemy attacked us on all sides with great strength and fierceness." [10] This part of his speech highlights the overwhelming challenges faced by the British forces, setting up a backdrop of adversity.

But then he shifts his focus to the British response to these dire conditions, framing it as a narrative of heroic defiance: "A miracle of deliverance, achieved by valour, by perseverance, by perfect discipline, by faultless service, by resource, by skill, by unconquerable fidelity, is manifest to us all."[11] This detailed assessment not only highlights the disparity in conditions but also underlines the heroism of the British forces. It serves to reinforce his call for continued resistance and bolsters the morale of both Parliament and the public.

By illustrating how the British forces managed to turn a near-certain defeat into a defensive victory, Churchill ensures his message isn't just informative but also motivational. His use of logos, through a meticulous recount of the events and their implications, logically leads to a conclusion that, despite the severe challenges, the spirit and resilience of the British forces can prevail.

This methodical breakdown, starting from acknowledging the potential disaster to detailing the remarkable turnaround thanks to the collective efforts of the military and civilians, effectively uses logos to build a compelling case for ongoing commitment and resistance against the aggressor.

This not only solidifies his ethos as a steadfast leader but also galvanizes the audience to embrace the ethos of resilience and determination in the face of adversity, leading to one conclusion: resist tyranny.

Pathos: Defiant Tone

Churchill's repeated use of the phrase "we shall fight"[12] functions as a rhythmic mantra that reinforces resilience and determination. Each iteration of the phrase builds on the last, layering intensity and driving home the message of unrelenting defiance.

One of the most famously quoted lines of this speech is: "We shall fight on the beaches, we shall fight on the landing grounds, we shall fight in the fields and in the streets, we shall fight in the hills; we shall never surrender."[13]

The deliberate escalation from beaches to streets to hills paints a vivid picture of an all-encompassing defense. This imagery instills a sense of inevitable victory, no matter the cost or terrain. The cadence of repetition, coupled with Churchill's authoritative delivery, struck a chord, converting fear of invasion into confidence in resistance.

Churchill also doesn't shy away from acknowledging Britain's desperate situation, but he uses this acknowledgment to ignite national pride. He speaks of Europe falling under the grip of Nazi tyranny, juxtaposing

Britain as the last bastion of European freedom: "Even though a large tract of Europe and many old and famous States have fallen or may fall into the grip of the Gestapo and all the odious apparatus of Nazi rule, we shall not flag nor fail. We shall go on to the end."[14]

He crafted this phrase to resonate emotionally by addressing the fears, hopes, and pride of his audience. It serves both as a declaration of action and a stirring rally cry that emotionally engages the listener, transforming fear into determination.

Churchill's vivid description of Europe under the Gestapo strikes a chord of urgency. By describing the "odious apparatus of Nazi rule," he makes the threat personal and visceral, and aims to evoke a gut-level reaction. Words he associates with Nazi rule like "odious" and "apparatus" are chosen for their negative connotations, invoking a deep-seated disgust and revulsion that make the threat feel immediate and personal, compelling the audience to respond emotionally, so they can act decisively.

The transition to "we shall not flag nor fail" appeals to Britain's sense of identity. It reminds the audience of their historical role as defenders of liberty, elevating their morale by framing them as the torchbearers of civilization.

Churchill also gives a message of hope against overwhelming odds: "We shall never surrender and even if, which I do not for a moment believe, this island or a large part of it were subjugated and starving, then our Empire beyond the seas, armed and guarded by the British Fleet, would carry on the struggle."[15]

Churchill acknowledges the gravity of the challenge. He uses phrases like "subjugated and starving," which provokes fear and desperation, but also resilience, as they outline the worst-case scenario yet reaffirm the commitment to fight regardless of circumstance.

Additionally, "Empire beyond the seas, armed and guarded by the British Fleet" conjures a sense of vastness and strength, providing a reassuring image of unyielding power and global reach that protects and perseveres, furthering a sense of security and hope. In doing this, Churchill recasts the situation as an opportunity for greatness. By vowing unwavering resistance, he elevates the struggle from a fight for survival to a noble cause.

Overcoming Common Fears

Churchill's speaking career demonstrates how individuals can face and triumph over fears that might otherwise silence them. Let's explore how he overcame three specific fears—having a speech impediment, being criticized, and being forgotten—and share lessons and applications for today's speakers.

Fear Of A Speech Impediment

Lesson: As a young boy, Churchill struggled with a noticeable lisp and a slight stutter, which made speaking publicly a major challenge. Instead of letting this fear define him, he approached it with sheer determination. Churchill tirelessly practiced enunciation and even hired a speech therapist to help him develop clarity and confidence. He would recite passages from great works, often over and over, until he could deliver them flawlessly. In *Speak Like Churchill, Stand Like Lincoln*, James C. Humes states: "Churchill developed techniques to overcome his lisp and stutter and make his delivery sparkle like diamonds."[16]

One technique was to introduce compelling words such as "unsordid" or "benignant" as opposites to sordid and malignant. Those words helped him to affect a deliberate stuttering pause. Often during preparations for delivering speeches, Churchill wrote out every word and rehearsed extensively, compensating for any of his speaking deficiencies with preparation and precision. His eventual mastery of public speaking was not inborn but earned.

Application

Churchill's example proves that dedicated effort can turn a perceived weakness into a strength for those with speech impediments. Practice speaking aloud daily, focus on clarity, and, when necessary, seek professional guidance. Remember, success is less about natural ability and more about persistence.

Exercise:

Identify one passage or speech you admire. Record yourself reading it aloud three times, focusing on enunciation and pacing. Compare the recordings and identify improvements you could make. Repeat this daily for one week to build confidence and elegance of delivery.

Fear Of Being Criticized

Lesson: Churchill faced immense criticism throughout his career, especially during his "wilderness years" in the 1930s, when his warnings about the Nazi threat were dismissed as alarmist. Many called him a "warmonger" and ridiculed his warnings as out of touch with the appeasement policies of the time.[17]

Instead of retreating, Churchill leaned into his convictions. He used criticism as motivation to refine his arguments, preparing meticulously for debates and speeches. His tenacity ensured that when the threat became undeniable, his voice rose above the noise of early doubters.

Application

Criticism is inevitable for those who take a stand, but it doesn't have to be paralyzing. Use it as feedback to fine-tune your message. Like Churchill, focus on clarity and evidence to win over your detractors and let your steadfastness earn you respect over time.

Exercise

Write a draft of a controversial or challenging speech. Share it with a trusted mentor or group and invite constructive feedback. Take note of repeated critiques and revise your speech to address the key points. Deliver the revised version and note the improvement in reception.

Fear Of Being Forgotten

Lesson: Churchill's speeches were designed both to inspire action in the moment and to resonate for generations. He understood that the weight of his words carried the potential to shape history. The phrases "we shall never surrender" from "We Shall Fight on the Beaches" and "This Was Their Finest Hour" endure as testaments to his understanding of rhetoric's power to leave a lasting impact.[18]

Churchill also wrote volumes of work, including his memoirs and histories, ensuring that his perspective on the events he lived through would be remembered and studied. This commitment to documenting his words and actions cemented his legacy.

Application

Think beyond the immediate impact of your words and focus on their long-term significance. Craft messages that reflect your principles and values and document your ideas for future generations. Your legacy is built not just in what you say, but in how those words endure.

Exercise

Reflect on a principle or value you deeply believe in. Write a brief speech or article articulating its importance and how it shapes your life. Share this with a group or even publish it, ensuring that your perspective becomes part of a lasting record.

Churchill's ability to face and conquer these fears—whether stemming from physical limitations, external criticism, or the fear of being forgotten—provides endless lessons. His life demonstrates that the path to impactful communication comes from perseverance, conviction, and crafting a legacy through deliberate and thoughtful words.

Personal Connection: When Britain Was Great

Every time I visit London, I make it a point to stand in front of the massive statue of Achilles in Hyde Park, while listening to Led Zeppelin's song "Achilles Last Stand." Then, I walk a few blocks to visit a nearby statue of Churchill. These figures, representing both mythic and real-life heroism, remind me of the power of steadfast leadership in battle and the lasting impact of courageous words.

Also, knowing American history, I bow my head and give thanks to the "Greatest Generation" of men who fulfilled Churchill's final sentence in his "We Shall Fight on the Beaches" speech. Churchill predicted that the land of his mother in the New World, the US, would help those allied countries in the Old World. They did so at a great cost. Churchill called upon those who "would carry on the struggle, until, in God's good time, the New World, with all its power and might, steps forth to the rescue and the liberation of the old."[19]

For those who stammer, Churchill is an excellent role model. He suffered from that affliction when young but found a way to overcome it. I highly recommend the 2010 film *The King's Speech*, in which the Churchill character tells King George that he himself stammered when young.[20] This is one of the best films that dramatizes how helpful a coach can be to a speaker's confidence and self-worth.

On the coaching front, I've worked with US veteran David Cyr, who was preparing to deliver a Memorial Day speech that he knew needed improvement. Cyr described two deaths: Private First-Class Jerod Dennis, killed by Al Qaeda in an ambush in 2003 in Afghanistan, and Sergeant Alexander Van Aalten, who lost his life saving Dutch soldiers from landmines in 2007.

During coaching sessions, we lightened the somber Memorial Day mood by starting with some dialogue of Cyr's daughter, Celia. She asks: "Daddy, what month do veterans like most?"

"I don't know, Celia."

"March."

Then we described the action where Cyr eluded three hand grenade blasts in one day.

When we got to the fallen soldiers, I had him speak much slower and give weight to each name. This will be a speech that Cyr will likely deliver not only on Memorial Day but on other occasions. Churchill's impact, particularly regarding how to speak about lives lost in battle against tyranny, was in the back of our minds as we worked together on this speech.

Because the heroism of Dunkirk that Churchill spoke about took place across the English Channel, it makes me think of one coaching client and friend, executive coach John Collingwood. He raised more than $108,000 for his native South African boys and girls club by swimming the Channel, starting in England, for fourteen hours. John passed out just within sight of the French coast. He was considered dead before being revived by medical staff. In his presentation about "doing what both terrifies and exhilarates you," I suggested that instead of chronologically telling the story, open with him being smacked back to life by the medical staff. Then, he could recount the story more dramatically while repeatedly asking the audience what goals they have that terrify and exhilarate them.

Lessons For Liberty's Leaders: Show Resolve, Preparation, And Courage

Churchill's "We Shall Fight on the Beaches" speech offers invaluable lessons for liberty's leaders in overcoming fears of speaking with an impediment, being criticized, and being forgotten. Through unwavering resolve, meticulous preparation, and moral courage, Churchill inspired not only his nation but also the world. His commanding use of ethos, logos, and pathos, coupled with his precise delivery, turned his words into an enduring beacon of defiance and hope during a time of great despair.

Churchill's legacy reminds us that great leaders do not shy away from challenges. Instead, they rise to meet them with unflinching determination, careful planning, and a profound sense of purpose. Reflecting on Churchill's own tribute to the Royal Air Force, we might say of liberty's defenders: "Never in the field of human conflict was so much owed by so many to so few."[21]

As the echoes of Churchill's wartime speeches faded, the mid-twentieth century brought new struggles for liberty and justice to the forefront. In the United States, the turbulent 1960s were marked by battles not against foreign tyranny but against the injustice of segregation. Just as Churchill called upon the British people to stand firm in the face of invasion, Martin Luther King, Jr. emerged to call upon Americans to live up to their original founding principles, wielding his own profound oratorical power.

CHAPTER 7

Content Of Character Versus Color Of Skin

Somewhere I read of the freedom of speech.
Somewhere I read of the freedom of press.
Somewhere I read that the greatness of America
is the right to protest for right.
DR. MARTIN LUTHER KING, JR. [1]

Even though the free, capitalist, individualist North defeated the slave-based, feudal, collectivist South in the US Civil War, that did not mean total justice was implemented from 1865 onward. There were lingering effects of racism via the Jim Crow laws and various forms of discrimination. Black heroes such as Booker T. Washington, George Washington Carver, and Madam C. J. Walker demonstrated that talent, ambition, and success came from moral character and choice rather than from accidental factors such as skin color. There could have been so much less harm to individuals and so many more societal advances had justice finally prevailed.

In 1947, Jackie Robinson broke the color barrier in Major League Baseball. It is difficult to calculate that impact in today's terms because baseball is not nearly as popular today as it was in American culture in the 1940s. Back then, white audiences saw something special on the field, and white owners knew they would have more successful teams if they went by talent instead of prejudice.

Robinson's nonviolent approach on and off the field impacted Dr. Martin Luther King, Jr.[2] During the 1950s, King's stature as a minister and leader of the Civil Rights movement gained steam and caused outrage for those stuck in collectivist, racist thinking. Abraham Lincoln paid the ultimate price in 1865 for his firm stance on preserving the Union and ending slavery. King had been threatened and jailed, but he continued to march forward until he, too, paid the ultimate price on April 4, 1968.

On August 28, 1963, during the historic March on Washington for Jobs and Freedom, King delivered one of the most iconic speeches in American history: his "I Have a Dream" speech.[3] At a time when the United States was still deeply divided by racial segregation and injustice, Dr. King's words touched hearts as a powerful call for equality, freedom, and nonviolent resistance. Standing before a crowd of over 250,000 people at the Lincoln Memorial, King articulated a vision of a better future, one where the promise of the American dream would be possible for all its citizens.

King's speech shows rhetorical brilliance. Grounded in Aristotle's ethos, logos, and pathos, King captured the hearts and minds of millions. Let's explore how he employed these tools to deliver a message of hope, dignity, and justice, understood as equality before the law. This ideal served as both a moral compass and a constitutional promise at the heart of his appeal.

Ethos: Moral Authority Rooted In History

King's speech begins with the words: "Five score years ago, a great American, in whose symbolic shadow we stand today, signed the Emancipation Proclamation." This allusion to Abraham Lincoln immediately anchors King within the American legacy of principled leadership and moral courage. By invoking Lincoln while speaking from the steps of the Lincoln Memorial, King situates his call for civil rights in the context of the nation's founding values. He makes clear that justice, in its truest sense, means equal treatment and protection under the law—a principle denied to African Americans despite the promises of emancipation. King's moral authority is further reinforced by his life of service as both a minister and a leader of the Civil Rights movement. His integrity, his seamless alignment of words and actions, compels trust, elevating his message beyond politics to a universal ethical standard.

King's credibility also stems from his personal cost in the fight for equality. He had been arrested, threatened, and targeted, yet his commitment to nonviolence remained steadfast. When he says, "We must forever conduct our struggle on the high plane of dignity and discipline," and "We must not allow our creative protest to degenerate into physical violence," he demonstrates the ethical commitment and leadership that have gained widespread respect. His experience with nonviolent resistance underscores his commitment to justice and discipline, elevating his moral standing and making his message resonate with greater authenticity.

King continues, "And so even though we face the difficulties of today and tomorrow, I still have a dream. It is a dream deeply rooted in the American dream." His personal resilience in the face of adversity and his commitment to the American dream exemplify his integrity and vision. By framing his dream as part of the broader American ideal, he appeals to shared national values. He demonstrates his belief in the nation's potential, further enhancing his ethos as a unifying and principled leader.

Logos: Historical Context And Metaphor: The "Bad Check"

Dr. King's use of a "bad check" metaphor on a defaulted promissory note illustrates the unfulfilled promises of American liberty: "America has given the Negro people a bad check, a check which has come back marked 'insufficient funds.'"⁴ This metaphor effectively communicates the injustice experienced by Black Americans while appealing to reason. The implicit argument is that America promised liberty to all of its citizens. Yet Black Americans remain excluded from the full exercise and protection of their individual rights under the Constitution. Therefore, the nation owes a moral and legal debt to fulfill its promise of liberty by ensuring that those rights are honored and upheld for all.

King structures his speech both logically and chronologically, outlining *past* injustices, the *present* urgency, and a vision for the *future*. His argument that "now is the time to make real the promises of democracy"⁵ presents a clear and rational call to action. By grounding his vision for equality in the principles of the Declaration of Independence and the US Constitution, he builds a strong case for civil rights as essential to America's identity.

King systematically addressed what had been wrong and why immediate action was needed, and then pointed to what that implies the future should look like: "Now is the time to rise from the dark and desolate valley of segregation to the sunlit path of racial justice."⁶ Here, King's logical structure transitions from identifying injustices to presenting an urgent call to action guided by a glorious vision.

The metaphor of rising from a "valley" to a "sunlit path" reinforces the logical progression toward justice. It reinforces the idea that achieving equality is the proper way to align with the principles of the United States' founding documents and national identity.

Pathos: Emotional Resonance

King's repeated refrain, "I have a dream," delivers an emotional crescendo that paints a hopeful vision for the future. Phrases such as "I have a dream that one day every valley shall be exalted, every hill and mountain shall be made low," inspire optimism and unity. This vivid imagery taps into the deep yearning for justice and equality, galvanizing them for continued action.

One of the most emotionally charged (and philosophically sound) moments in his speech is this line: "I have a dream that my four little children will one day live in a nation where they will not be judged by the color of their skin but by the content of their character."[7] This statement has become one of the defining phrases of the Civil Rights movement, and it encapsulates King's vision of a just society.

This also appeals to various emotions in his audience such as aspiration and empathy. The aspirational aspect of King's dream regarding his children resonates with any parent's desire for their children's better future, making his aspirations universal and deeply personal for his listeners. By invoking the image of his children, King personalizes the struggle against racial discrimination, making it more relatable and stirring empathy among his listeners. It shifts the abstract concept of civil rights into a concrete, understandable frame that touches on family love and protection.

King is not merely condemning racism: He's also offering a better alternative, a world where justice prevails. The emotional appeal is not only to those who have experienced prejudice, but also to those who believe in the fundamental principles of liberty and equality. By asking the audience to imagine their offspring being able to sit together and value one another as unique persons, King moves his listeners to expand their application of justice beyond racial boundaries.

Repetition and geographic specificity evoke a powerful sense of unity, as King achieves with these words: "Let freedom ring from every hill and molehill of Mississippi . . . From every mountainside, let freedom ring."[8] The imagery of freedom ringing across the nation stirs pride, hope, and a sense of shared destiny.

In his 1931 book, *The Epic of America*, James Truslow Adams defines the American dream as "a dream of social order in which each man and each woman shall be able to attain to the fullest stature of which they are innately capable."[9] King's speech expands on this vision, demanding that the American dream be accessible to all, regardless of race.

Patriotism is as much about appealing to emotions as it is to values. Using the American dream as a touchstone allows King to rouse patriotic sentiment and inspire everyone to become better Americans.

Overcoming Common Fears

King's words and actions offer important lessons for overcoming fears that many speakers face, including the fear of having nothing important to say, the fear of speaking freely, and the fear of stating the obvious and being ignored. Let's explore how King's approach addresses each of these fears.

Fear Of Having Nothing Important To Say

Lesson: Speak with purpose and values. King's speeches demonstrate that having something important to say is less about possessing unique insights and more about speaking with conviction and aligning your words with universal truths. King didn't invent the ideals of justice and equality, but he brought them to life through his unique voice, perspective, and passion.

In his "I Have a Dream" speech, King draws on well-known principles such as the Declaration of Independence's promise of equality: "We hold these truths to be self-evident, that all men are created equal." He then makes these timeless truths personal and relevant, applying them to the struggles of Black Americans in the 1960s.

─**Application**─────────────────────────────

If you fear having nothing important to say, focus on connecting universal values to personal and current experiences. King's example shows that powerful messages often come from revisiting foundational truths and expressing how they feel meaningful in your life and cause.

Exercise

Write down three universal truths or values that resonate deeply with you (e.g., choice, justice, freedom). Then, connect each value to a personal experience or a current event. Practice crafting a two-to-three-minute speech around one of these connections to articulate its importance.

Fear Of Speaking Freely

Lesson: Moral courage fuels free speech. King faced extreme risks when he spoke out against racial injustice. From imprisonment to threats against his life, King knew the consequences of challenging the status quo. Yet he believed that remaining silent would be a great betrayal of his principles.

In his "Letter from a Birmingham Jail," he writes: "We will reach the goal of freedom in Birmingham and all over the nation, because the goal of America is freedom."[10] Here, King summons American integrity and justifies speaking freely by making it a moral necessity, showing that silence in the face of injustice perpetuates harm.

Application

If you fear speaking freely, take inspiration from King's conviction that truth and justice are worth the risk. Think about the advances achieved because of what he was willing to say. Recognize that your voice can be a catalyst for change and that silence often comes at a greater cost to yourself and others.

Exercise

Identify an issue or topic you've been hesitant to speak about but feel strongly about. Write a short letter to yourself explaining why this topic matters and what positive change your voice could bring. Then, practice expressing your thoughts aloud to a trusted friend or mentor.

Fear Of Stating The Obvious And Being Ignored

Lesson: King's rhetoric often stated truths that many already knew, but he reframed them in a way that made them urgent and impossible to ignore. For example, the inequality Black Americans faced, particularly in the South, was evident to anyone paying attention, but King made it emotionally compelling by emphasizing its moral and practical implications.

In "I Have a Dream," King repeats the refrains, "I have a dream," and "Let freedom ring," at least eight times each with a rhythmic cadence. By using repetition, urgency, and broad language, King transforms what might seem like an obvious truth into a rallying cry for immediate action.

Application

If you fear stating the obvious, focus on presenting well-known truths in a way that energizes your audience. Use repetition, vivid imagery, and emotional appeals to make familiar ideas hit home with new significance.

Exercise

Choose a well-known goal (e.g., "I will pursue the American dream" or "Let freedom ring"). Rewrite this principle in your own words, adding vivid imagery or personal anecdotes to make it more impactful. Then, try repeating it as a refrain, grounding it in specific, tangible examples each time. Practice delivering it with conviction to a small group of friends or colleagues.

Personal Connection: Individualism And Collectivism

I grew up in New York City and witnessed acts of violence committed by one racial group against another, and it gave me pause to look for the underlying cause of this hostility. Learning that all races have individuals who are good and bad, the notion of judging people as a collective vanished. That's when I realized that King's appeal to the "content of character" rather than the "color of skin" was fundamentally about embracing individualism. One of my signature keynote speeches is centered on the American dream. I make it a point to emphasize that King's dream was rooted in that premise.

You might not know that King was the sixteenth of eighteen speakers the day he delivered his most famous speech. Keep that in mind if you feel lost in a crowd at a program with so many others and want to be remembered. One person's voice can memorably rise above all the others. That voice could be yours.

Some might not be aware of the impromptu nature of part of this speech. At one point, while King was reading from his script, he heard singer Mahalia Jackson say, "Tell them about the dream, Martin."[11] King pivoted right then and there, moving into the immortal segment of his presentation. So be ready to change immediately if there is a better way to give your audience an unforgettable experience. That's why I practice impromptu speaking at Toastmasters club and improv group meetings.

Another personal connection happened a few years ago when Carrie-Ann and I visited some friends in Atlanta. We hiked to the top of Stone Mountain. On our way down, we saw a beautiful work of art that, on closer inspection, quickly turned my stomach. It turned out to be a large memorial that portrays three Confederate leaders: Jefferson Davis, Robert E. Lee, and Stonewall Jackson. The figures are 90 feet by 190 feet on a carved oval background larger than a football field. Sadly, the glorification of these figures is part of American history. Right then, I knew what King's speech meant when he said, "Let freedom ring from Stone Mountain in Georgia."

One of my coaching students, Sumaira Waseem, is a pro-liberty Muslim who lives in Pakistan. She is a division coordinator for Afghanistan and Pakistan with South Asia Students for Liberty. Sumaira heroically speaks out in a place where freedoms are often squashed by authorities. She's also on the lookout for inspiration. After my presentation at the Nairobi summit in 2024, she said:

> I attended Mr. Robert Begley's session, this summit in Nairobi, which was about the big seven speakers who were very celebrated and known for their cogent speeches. But what the session really

explored was why their speeches endured all these years. It was because they were able to maintain purposeful, engaging, and hopeful speeches that had content and centered around a better future for everyone. And so if you wish to compose a speech that is able to inspire others, then you'd be able to nurture the next generation of leaders as well.[12]

This highlights the core principle that most memorable and influential speeches are those that not only deliver content effectively but also resonate with audiences on a deeper emotional level. Such speeches are distinguished by their ability to envision a better future, thereby inspiring others to act and potentially nurturing the next generation of leaders.

The essence of this approach is that effective communication should serve a transformative purpose, aiming to motivate and guide others toward positive change. This is a powerful reminder for any speaker that the true measure of a speech's success is the lasting impact on its audience and its ability to cultivate leadership and progress.

Here are some additional insights that can help us from King's brilliant speech.

Use Of Vivid Imagery

King's ability to paint vivid mental pictures enabled his audience to see the world he envisioned. This imagery made abstract ideas tangible, encouraging a deeper emotional connection. King's imagery created snapshots of his dream that hit a chord with his audience.

Consider this passage: "I have a dream that one day the sons of former slaves and the sons of former slave owners will be able to sit down together at the table of brotherhood."[13] This metaphor of a shared table encapsulates reconciliation and equality in a way that is both simple and profound. It evokes a future where differences are set aside in favor of unity and mutual respect.

Another example is "Let freedom ring," from the famous "My Country 'Tis of Thee" song, which he recites first. He then repeats the expression eight times: "Let freedom ring from the prodigious hilltops of New Hampshire . . . Let freedom ring from the curvaceous slopes of California."[14] This geographical imagery creates a vivid mental map of a unified nation, further reinforcing the idea that freedom should echo from every corner of the country.

Commanding Presence

One can watch King's speech on YouTube[15] to see how his physical delivery played a crucial role in amplifying his words. The *way* he spoke was as compelling as what he said. King's delivery was calculated. His pacing allowed the audience to absorb his words, while his resonant voice carried authority and emotional depth.

He used pauses strategically, giving weight to key points and allowing his audience time to reflect. For instance, before delivering the refrain, "I have a dream," he would pause, creating anticipation and heightening the impact of his words.

Additionally, his posture—standing tall and exuding confidence—added to his commanding presence. He used gestures to emphasize points, but never excessively, ensuring they complemented rather than distracted from his message.

A Lesson For Liberty's Leaders: Embrace Universal Values

King's "I Have a Dream" speech delivers a message rooted in universal values. Practicing and refining his oratory skills and speaking with moral courage, King created a speech that not only galvanized a movement but also secured his place in history. His skillful use of ethos, logos, and pathos, combined with his strategic delivery, ensured that his words would echo through the ages as a beacon of hope and justice. King's example teaches us as leaders that with conviction, preparation, and a commitment to truth, our words can inspire others and leave an enduring legacy.

As the Civil Rights movement gained momentum, uniting people under the banner of justice and equality, another voice rose to challenge racism, which Ayn Rand called "the most primitive form of collectivism."[16] Rand, an unapologetic advocate of individualism and rational self-interest, declared, "I know that I am challenging the cultural tradition of two and a half thousand years."[17]

CHAPTER 8

A Philosophy For Living On Earth

Speak on any scale open to you ... You can never tell when your words will reach the right mind at the right time. You will see no immediate results—but it is of such activities that public opinion is made.

AYN RAND[1]

In the tumultuous, emotion-dominated 1960s, against a backdrop of cultural, political, and social upheaval, Ayn Rand was a voice of reason, speaking out on college campuses about the heroic human spirit. While Martin Luther King, Jr. and other leaders such as Robert F. Kennedy were assassinated, Rand lived to present a radical, idealistic view of man and human potential.

Rand's novels *The Fountainhead* (1943) and *Atlas Shrugged* (1957) feature characters like Howard Roark, John Galt, and Dagny Taggart, who were unlike any other literary figures. Roark exemplifies Rand's ideal man, an independent thinker committed to his vision and values, embodying her philosophy of individualism and self-reliance. John Galt and Dagny Taggart embody Rand's principles of rational self-interest, capitalism, and the pursuit of happiness. They each dramatize Rand's virtues of rationality, honesty, productiveness, and pride.

111

Rand also acknowledged Aristotle's foundational influence on her thinking, particularly in the realm of logic and reasoning, calling him "the greatest of all philosophers."[2]

Despite her thick Russian accent, about which she was self-conscious, Rand saw value in public speaking. During the 1940s, she vocally promoted Wendell Willkie's anti-New Deal policies in New York City. In her biographical study *Who Is Ayn Rand?*, Barbara Branden explains how Rand "spoke on street corners, often to vocally hostile crowds. Once, a heckler demanded: 'Who are you to talk about America? You're a foreigner!' She calmly answered, 'That's right. I chose to be an American. What did you do besides having been born?' The crowd laughed and applauded—and the heckler was silent."[3]

During the 1960s, Rand gained traction and became an iconic speaker, appearing three times as a guest on Johnny Carson's *The Tonight Show*.[4] Between 1961 and 1981, she was invited nine times to speak at Boston's Ford Hall Forum. She drew sellout crowds, who attended both to hear the intensity of her ideas and watch her handle the often-hostile question-and-answer period.

By the 1970s, Rand had cut back on speaking engagements aside from the Ford Hall Forum until the United States Military Academy at West Point sent her a letter: "We sought you out because we think you can fire a young man's imagination as well as kindle his thoughts."[5]

In Shoshana Milgram's talk, "Behind the Scenes: Ayn Rand's West Point Lecture (1974–2024)," she describes why Rand accepted this invitation. It goes back to World War II: While the Nazis were burning books, Americans were publishing them. Rand received many letters from soldiers on the battlefield, who considered her book *The Fountainhead* as a lifeline. Also, although Rand disagreed with the Vietnam War, she did not blame the actual soldiers (who were merely pawns in a larger game) but considered them heroes who were hungry for recognition.

On March 6, 1974, Rand delivered "Philosophy: Who Needs It" at the United States Military Academy at West Point.[6] In this speech, Rand argued that philosophy is an essential, unavoidable guide for life, shaping everything from values to actions. She challenged her audience of future military leaders to choose their philosophy consciously.

We'll look at this speech through the lens of Aristotle's rhetorical principles of ethos, logos, and pathos.

Ethos: Establishing Credibility Through Philosophy And Experience

Rand's credibility was rooted in her status as a novelist and philosopher, with best-selling works like *Atlas Shrugged* and *The Fountainhead*, as well as the achievement of developing her own philosophy, which she called Objectivism.

In her speech, she builds her ethos by demonstrating her expertise and grounding her message in philosophical rigor. Rand declares, "Philosophy studies the *fundamental* nature of existence, of man, and of man's relationship to existence . . . In the realm of cognition, the special sciences are the trees, but philosophy is the soil which makes the forest possible."[7]

By framing philosophy as the root of all human knowledge and progress, she asserts her authority as a thinker who has deeply explored and mastered these subjects. This statement establishes her as someone with philosophical rigor who is uniquely qualified to address the graduating cadets.

Rand also makes a personal connection to freedom. She reinforced her ethos by drawing on her life story, mentioning her escape from Soviet

Russia. Her life experience under totalitarian oppression and subsequent embrace of American freedom gave her an authentic voice when discussing the importance of philosophy in defending liberty.

She explains, "Since I came from a country guilty of the worst tyranny on earth, I am particularly able to appreciate the meaning, the greatness, and the supreme value of that which you are defending."[8]

Her life story resonates with the values of the cadets at West Point, underscoring her sincerity and alignment with the ideals of life, liberty, and the pursuit of happiness. Rand's audience trusted that she was committed to their shared ideals, ones they had pledged to protect with their lives if necessary.

Logos: Logical Structure And Arguments

Rand demonstrated that philosophy is unavoidable and that philosophical principles underpin every aspect of human decision-making, from personal ethics to political systems: "A philosophic system is an integrated view of existence. As a human being, you have no choice about the fact that you need a philosophy. Your only choice is whether you define your philosophy by a conscious, rational, disciplined process of thought and scrupulously logical deliberation—or let your subconscious accumulate a junk heap of unwarranted conclusions."[9]

By linking abstract philosophy to concrete examples, such as ethics and military conduct, Rand made the subject relevant to the military cadets. They are often faced with complex moral dilemmas where the right course of action is not solely dictated by orders or manuals but requires a deep understanding of ethical principles. A consciously chosen philosophy helps ensure their actions are both legally right and morally justified, thus ensuring the integrity and honor that military service demands.

Rand also used logic to connect philosophy to effective leadership by demonstrating how it shapes moral clarity. She argued that leaders cannot act effectively without understanding the principles guiding their choices, especially when confronting opponents who want to undermine or even destroy them: "A battle of this kind requires special weapons. It has to be fought with a full understanding of your cause, a full confidence in yourself, and the fullest certainty of the *moral* rightness of both. Only philosophy can provide you with those weapons."[10]

Rand warned that without a clear philosophical grounding, leaders are susceptible to manipulation and coercion by those well-defined, though destructive, ideologies. This can lead to strategic and ethical blunders in military operations and leadership, making leaders and their troops vulnerable to propaganda and moral compromises.

Rand also linked ethics to practical action: "Ethics, or morality, defines a code of values to guide man's choices and actions—the choices and actions that determine the course of his life."[11] She explained that before a person can act effectively, one must understand one's values and the principles underpinning them. She explained that ethics outlines a set of values and actions.

For cadets, understanding their own values and the principles behind them is essential for navigating both everyday choices and broader career-defining moments. This understanding equips them with the tools to evaluate their actions and the consequences, ensuring their decisions align with their long-term personal and professional goals.

As a result, her audience sees how ethics directly affects their everyday decisions and their broader life goals. Rand portrays philosophy as an indispensable tool that ensures they lead with integrity and purpose, vital for their success in both military and civilian spheres.

Pathos: Pursuit Of Joy And Appeal To Sense Of Pride

Rand emotionally connects with her audience by presenting a vision of life centered on the pursuit of happiness: "Should man's primary concern be a quest for joy—or an escape from suffering? Should man hold self-fulfillment—or self-destruction—as the goal of his life?"[12]

These questions directly challenge the cadets to reflect deeply on their personal and professional aspirations. By juxtaposing positive aspirations (joy, self-fulfillment) with negative outcomes (suffering, self-destruction) Rand encourages the cadets to consciously choose a path that leads toward personal achievement and satisfaction.

This stark contrast likely stirs a desire to pursue a life that transcends mere survival or the avoidance of discomfort, aiming instead for a life enriched with purpose and joy. Her words evoke hope and a sense of possibility, appealing to the audience's desire for a meaningful existence.

Rand's emphasis on self-fulfillment challenges her audience to take ownership of their principles and actions, rejecting passivity or reliance on others. She then draws a parallel between a proud, disciplined control of their body and of their mind:

Nothing is given to man automatically, neither knowledge, nor self-confidence, nor inner serenity, nor the right way to use his mind. Every value he needs has to be discovered, learned and acquired—even the proper posture of his body . . . I have always admired the proud posture of West Point graduates, a posture that projects man in proud, disciplined control of his body. Well, philosophical training gives man the proper *intellectual* posture—a proud, disciplined control of his mind.[13]

Rand's assertion here connects directly with the cadets' rigorous training environment, where achievement through hard work and personal discipline is paramount. The phrase "nothing is given" resonates with their understanding that valuable traits and success must be earned, which reinforces their ongoing effort. This both motivates and validates their arduous journey toward leadership and excellence.

Rand effectively draws a parallel between the visible, physical discipline that is the hallmark of military training and the less visible, intellectual discipline that philosophy requires. By using the word "posture," she bridges the tangible concept familiar to cadets with an abstract concept, enhancing their appreciation of mental discipline.

This comparison both elevates the importance of philosophical thought and instills pride in their intellectual pursuits, similar to their pride in physical fitness and bearing. By drawing the parallel to intellectual development, Rand raises philosophy to the same level as their military training, inspiring them to see philosophy as an essential component of their growth as leaders.

Finally, Rand expresses profound admiration for the cadets and their mission: "There is a kind of quiet radiance associated in my mind with the name West Point—because you have preserved the spirit of those original founding principles and you are their symbol."[14]

This heartfelt acknowledgment of their dedication and honor connects their individual efforts to a broader, noble cause, making them feel that their work contributes to the preservation of freedom and human dignity. The term "quiet radiance" evokes a feeling of profound glow of pride, linking their daily efforts to the lofty ideals and historic legacy of West Point.

Through these carefully chosen words and phrases, Rand not only communicates her philosophical ideals (which she informally calls "a philosophy for living on earth"[15]) but also effectively engages the cadets' emotions, inspiring them to see philosophy as essential to their personal growth and professional effectiveness. This approach ensures that her message is not only heard but felt, nurturing a deep connection with her audience and encouraging them to embrace philosophy as a critical tool in their leadership arsenal.

Summary

By illustrating how principles guide action, Rand ties philosophy to practical decision-making. Her argument appeals to the cadets' sense of duty and their role as defenders of freedom, reinforcing the importance of aligning their actions with rational and ethical principles.

Rand's speech exemplifies the power of combining ethos, logos, and pathos to convey a compelling vision of a purposeful, values-driven life. Through her intellectual rigor, emotional appeals, and personal connection, she inspires her audience to embrace philosophy as a guide for living with integrity and joy.

Overcoming Common Fears

In *Philosophy: Who Needs It*, Rand offers valuable lessons for overcoming three common fears: the fear of public speaking, the fear of being heckled and losing focus, and the fear of being misunderstood.

Fear Of Public Speaking

Lesson: Despite her thick Russian accent, Rand showed that preparation and authenticity could overcome fear of public speaking. She meticulously prepared her speeches, often delivering "spoken articles" with carefully crafted arguments. Her authenticity, grounded in her personal story of escaping Soviet Russia and choosing to become an American, gave her speech a unique appeal.

---Application---

Develop your speech with a clear structure and practice it many times until you are confident. Even if using a script, make sure the delivery feels natural and heartfelt. Also, share authentic anecdotes or insights that ground your speech in reality and make you relatable to your audience. This personal connection often reduces fear as it shifts the focus from performance to communication.

Exercise

Write a two-minute personal story that ties into your speech topic. Practice delivering it aloud five times, focusing on pacing and tone. Record your delivery on video and review it to identify areas for improvement. Reflect on how sharing your personal story makes the message more engaging and authentic.

Fear Of Being Heckled And Losing Focus

Lesson: Turn challenges into opportunities. Rand faced hecklers many times. For instance, as noted above, when challenged about her right to speak on American issues as a foreigner, she turned the criticism into an opportunity to strengthen her ethos: "That's right. I *chose* to be an American. What did you do besides having been born?" Her calm and witty response not only silenced her heckler but also won over the audience, demonstrating her ability to maintain focus under pressure.

Application

Anticipate challenges by preparing before every speech. Consider potential criticisms or interruptions and think about how you might respond to them constructively. Also, a lighthearted but pointed response can often disarm critics and redirect the audience's attention to your message. And finally, stay calm and focus on the larger goal of your speech. Remind yourself that a single interruption does not define the entire presentation.

Exercise

Write down three potential criticisms or questions you might face during a speech. For each, craft a concise, respectful response that reaffirms your message. Practice these responses with a friend acting as a heckler. Focus on maintaining composure and redirecting the conversation back to your main points.

Fear Of Being Misunderstood

Lesson: Be as clear as possible and make sure you have a logical structure. Rand's ability to present complex philosophical ideas in a clear, logical manner helped her reduce misunderstandings. In her speech at West Point, she framed abstract concepts with concrete examples, such as equating philosophical discipline with the cadets' proud military posture. By anchoring her ideas in relatable analogies, she minimized the risk of misinterpretation.

Application

Communicate your message using clear, simple language and examples to simplify complex ideas. Avoid unnecessary jargon that might confuse your audience. Pause for questions or feedback to ensure your message is landing as intended. Reiterate your key points to help with clarity and understanding.

Exercise

Take a complex idea you plan to discuss in your next speech and write a thirty-second explanation using simple, clear language. Then, create one analogy or example to illustrate your point. Practice delivering it to someone unfamiliar with the topic and ask for feedback on clarity and understanding. Refine your explanation based on their input.

Personal Connection: The Arc Of Heroism

My personal trajectory of hero worship began with Spider-Man (cocreated by Stan Lee and Rand-influenced Steve Ditko), moved to Greek mythology (Prometheus means "forethought"), and elevated with Ayn Rand's literary heroes who use reason as their guide to action. I had read Rand's *Anthem* by age sixteen and *The Fountainhead* and *Atlas Shrugged* by age eighteen.

Rand's influence led me to believe that happiness is the purpose of life, that my independence matters, and that the art I admire should dramatize heroism and give me spiritual fuel. I'd often quote Rand and emphasize my individualism (as number eight of nine kids), and my mother would comment, "Robert is in that Ayn Rand phase." It's not a "phase," because it's a "philosophy for living on earth"[16] throughout one's life.

One of my proudest achievements was being invited by the Public Broadcasting System to discuss *Atlas Shrugged* for their Great American Read[17] program. As mentioned in chapter 2, my own Manhattan cable TV show in the 1990s, *The Voice of Reason*, was named after one of Rand's posthumous essay collections.[18] Her ideas on independence, heroism, and benevolence continue to shape my work as a speaker and coach.

As a speaking coach for decades, I've often seen an imbalance of logos at the expense of ethos and pathos when speakers discuss Rand's ideas. I have worked hard to avoid that in my own presentations so that they can leave lasting impressions. For instance, in April 2024, after I spoke in Tbilisi, Georgia, about the heroism in Rand's aesthetics, coaching client and *Reason* assistant editor Jack NiCastro described what I've felt for decades: "Robert's presentation vividly described how Ayn Rand's fiction, Ayn Rand's art provides us moral exemplars that we can use to lead flourishing lives."[19]

This short testimonial, focusing on the application of Rand's philosophical themes through her art, highlights the transformative potential of literature on personal development. It suggests that engaging deeply with Rand's work can equip individuals with the philosophical foundation necessary to navigate life's challenges with moral clarity and purpose, ultimately leading to a more fulfilled and principled existence.

After a presentation I gave in the summer of 2024 in Nairobi, Kenya, using Aristotle's principles of rhetoric, one student explained how she used those ideas to help her team win a debate competition. I'll let Amanda de Vasconcellos speak for herself:

> Robert gave a presentation two days ago about logos, pathos, and ethos. They are the principles of giving a great speech. And I feel like I've always been a logos person, a person of ideas, of going from A to B to C logically and just expecting it to work. But I

know it doesn't work like that. However, it is hard to actually put into practice the ethos, the credibility, and the pathos, which is emotion. But I think that in this debate competition I was able to do both, because it was so thoroughly explained and so repeated to us during the feedback sessions by Robert and many others of the judges how we should be always trying to show up, who we are and not just what we believe in. And through that we show that our ideas hold some gravitas and also that we truly care about what we are talking about, so I'm really grateful, Robert. You truly helped us win this debate competition.[20]

Not only do these kinds of testimonials warm my heart, but they also reinforce my coaching methodology, which integrates ethos, logos, and pathos in ways that can enhance debate skills while instilling a deeper understanding of how to communicate one's authenticity and passion effectively, which can lead to victory.

We've seen how Rand's ideas moved US cadets at West Point. How about leaders in the New York Police Department? I corresponded with long-time friend, entrepreneur, and author, Dan Modell, who had one of the toughest jobs in the world before retiring a few years ago—lieutenant with the NYPD. The topics were stress, leadership, and ethics at the NYPD. Modell said: "Rand's identification and defense of reason as man's essential 'means of survival' framed the cognitive background that carried me through my career in policing."[21]

Modell describes confronting intense situations where maintaining a focus on "the reality that confronts you, the possibilities that circumstances present" was crucial for navigating the volatile situations that arise in New York policing.[22] This application of reason, especially in high-stress encounters with armed criminals, has the hallmarks of logos.

Reflecting on the relationship between individualism and leadership, Modell taps into pathos by understanding the emotional aspects of leadership. He emphasizes the value of recognizing individual contributions and creative freedom: "Individualism was the guiding core of my perspective as a leader." He fostered an environment where "if there was a crime condition and an officer had an idea of how to address it, he had my ear and we would talk it through." This approach underpins his belief that leadership is about enabling each person to "achieve 'the best within him,'" echoing Rand's focus on personal excellence.[23] This methodology not only appeals to the personal pride and fulfillment of his officers but also resonates emotionally with their desire for respect and autonomy in their roles.

On the topic of ethos and credibility, Modell critiques common leadership failures and underscores the importance of accountability: "I have noticed that managers make a common error that undermines credibility: they refuse to acknowledge mistakes and take responsibility for them." He shares his own practice: "When I made an error in judgment, I acknowledged it, apologized, and signaled my intention to do better going forward."[24] This approach not only built trust but also ensured that his leadership was respected and followed, establishing a stronger foundation for ethical leadership.

These elements of ethos, logos, and pathos combine to provide a comprehensive view of Dan Modell's leadership philosophy and how it has been shaped by the principles of Ayn Rand, thereby making a compelling case for the practical application of these philosophical principles in law enforcement.

Lessons For Liberty's Leaders: Reason Rules

Ayn Rand's *Philosophy: Who Needs It* is a guide to overcoming fears of public speaking, being heckled and losing focus, and of being misunderstood—not just for West Point graduates, but for everyone. By rigorously preparing, standing by her convictions, and promoting a life guided by reason, Rand left an indelible mark on the world.

Rand's use of ethos, logos, and pathos, combined with her passionate delivery, ensured that her ideas would endure and inspire future generations. For today's liberty leaders, her example teaches us to speak boldly, live purposefully, and leave a lasting impact.

In anticipation of the next chapter, which emphasizes the effort to bring freedom to a largely unfree part of the globe—the African continent—many people are bravely upholding Rand's ideas there. One hero is Edgard Mugenzi, from Burundi, a country bordering Rwanda, Tanzania, and the Democratic Republic of Congo. Mugenzi is a doctor who advocates human rights, health, and well-being. He also teaches Rand's philosophy to students.

After hearing my presentation in Nairobi, through a beaming smile, Mugenzi said, "Robert taught us Objectivism with practical examples, which helped me personally to understand the ideas more. I'm really happy to see how students understand easier the morality of objectivity when we teach them with practical examples."[25] By utilizing practical examples to teach, Mugenzi effectively communicates the morality of objectivity, making complex philosophical concepts more accessible and impactful to students in Africa.

Edgard also looks up to another passionate and eloquent woman who has taken up the mantle of defending the freedom to create values: Magatte Wade. While Rand used philosophy to champion the moral and practical foundations of capitalism, Wade has focused on the real-world impact of free enterprise in transforming lives and lifting nations out of poverty.

CHAPTER 9

From Poverty To Prosperity

Businesses create jobs. Jobs pay people money.
And when Africans have money, they will no longer be poor.

MAGATTE WADE[1]

When people think of Africa, they often picture a vast wilderness, conjure images from *The Lion King*, or recall headlines of apartheid in South Africa. Others imagine poverty-stricken villages, with sick children swatting flies away from their faces. But is any of this a fair assessment of a vast continent comprising fifty-four countries?

Africa is a continent rich in natural resources, yet most of its people still face widespread poverty despite receiving billions in foreign aid. What does this say about the system in place? Is it possible that foreign aid has inadvertently damaged the dignity of African people? What if, instead of relying on aid, African countries embraced free markets to uplift their communities?

Enter Magatte Wade—a Senegal-born entrepreneur (founder of Adina World Beat Beverages, Tiossan, and Skin Is Skin) and tireless advocate of economic freedom in Africa. I've had the privilege of meeting her; she is a force of nature.

In her August 2017 TEDGlobal talk, "Why It's Too Hard to Start a Business in Africa—and How to Change It,"[2] Wade shines a light on the systemic barriers that stifle entrepreneurship across the continent. Drawing from her own experience, Wade dissects the overregulation, corruption, and lack of infrastructure that hinder business growth. Her talk is both a diagnosis of the problems and a passionate call to action for reform.

Ethos: Personal Authority And Authentic Experience

Wade's ethos is firmly established by her experience as a successful entrepreneur. Her personal journey lends credibility to her message and positions her as a trusted advocate of African entrepreneurship.

In her presentation, Wade starts by saying, "So, I have this attitude in life: something is wrong, find a way to fix it. And that's why I started the business that I start."[3] This line reveals Wade's ethos as a proactive problem-solver whose credibility stems from aligning her values with entrepreneurial action.

Then Wade shares a poignant moment that underscores her moral authority and personal connection to the issue. She recounts a staffer named Yahara, who said, "I'm crying because I had come to believe . . . that maybe, yet, maybe we are inferior." That broke Wade's heart at first, but also gave her hope when Yahara concluded, "But now I know that I am not the problem. It is the environment in which I live, that's my problem."[4]

This statement encapsulates her deep understanding of the systemic barriers hindering African entrepreneurship. It highlights her commitment to addressing these challenges not just as an observer but as someone who has navigated and confronted them personally.

By sharing such experiences, Wade positions herself as both a critic of flawed systems and a proactive agent for change.

By highlighting her dual perspective—having succeeded in both African and Western contexts—Wade establishes herself as highly qualified to compare and contrast the two systems and understand what hinders African entrepreneurs and allows American entrepreneurs to flourish. Her credibility is heightened further by her success as the founder of skin care brand Tiossan, which ties African traditions to global markets, showcasing her ability to translate African potential into reality at the international level.

Logos: Economic Analysis Of Barriers

Wade constructs a data-driven argument to expose the structural barriers that stifle African entrepreneurship. Her talk moves systematically from identifying the problems to proposing actionable solutions.

She gives striking examples to illustrate the inefficiencies of African bureaucracy: "I have to pay a 45% tariff on everything that comes in . . . I can't find new, finished cardboard . . . because the distributors are not going to come here to start their business . . . So right now I have to mobilize $3,000 worth of cardboard in my warehouse, so that I can have cardboard, and they won't arrive for another five weeks."[5] In contrast, starting a business and getting supplies affordably and reliably takes just days in many developed countries. This stark comparison highlights the gigantic problem that creates insurmountable barriers for entrepreneurs: overregulation.

By grounding her critique in hard numbers, Wade makes the statistics speak for themselves. She shows how the regulatory state impedes business creation. Her use of quantitative evidence appeals to her audience's logic and reinforces the urgency of reform.

Wade transitions from identifying problems to proposing actionable solutions, emphasizing deregulation to uphold a pro-entrepreneurial system that creates jobs and can lead Africa out of poverty. She asks, "Where do jobs come from? Businesses, thank you . . . then maybe for a second we should focus on making it easy for a small-business person to start and run their own business?"[6] She concludes with a take-charge attitude: "Get out of my way. You let people like me do our job, we create all these jobs we need, and then Africa becomes a very prosperous country that it's designed to be."[7]

In other words, it's not enough to complain or beg for handouts. Just lift the regulations, end the corruption, and Africa will flourish. Wade's rational approach appeals to policymakers and international investors, making her solutions practical.

Pathos: Care And Hope

Wade's talk, though data-driven, carries an emotional appeal that elevates her message and allows her to connect deeply with her audience—so much so that they leap to their feet to give her a standing ovation at the end of her speech.

In her book, *The Heart of A Cheetah*, Wade paints a vivid picture of the consequences of Africa's entrepreneurial barriers: "We will stay stuck in an endless cycle of poverty until these chains are finally broken and our markets are set free."[8] This statement taps into the audience's empathy, highlighting the deep connection between economic freedom and human dignity. It calls on them to recognize that bureaucratic red tape is both inefficient and oppressive. Until these barriers are removed, opportunity will stay out of reach for millions with the will to build but not the freedom to begin.

By framing the issue in terms of real lives affected, Wade shifts the discussion from abstract economics to actual human suffering. Her emotional appeal compels the audience to see the urgency of the problem not only as a matter of policy but as a moral imperative.

Wade's vision of Africa offers a fundamental choice: "If they don't have an outlook in life, they are going for a revolution . . . Or the second way it can go is, all this happens peacefully, productively, and everything is good."[9] This pathos-laden warning evokes fear and hope by offering a clear fork in the road: peaceful reform leading to flourishing or inevitable unrest leading to violence.

Wade's passion is infectious. Her vision contrasts sharply with the grim realities she describes, creating a powerful emotional arc in her talk. This balance between acknowledging challenges and inspiring hope motivates her audience to believe that change is possible and to take action to support it.

In her TEDGlobal talk, Wade demonstrates the art of persuasion by seamlessly blending ethos, logos, and pathos. Her credibility as an entrepreneur and advocate (ethos), her data-driven argument (logos), and her heartfelt connection to Africa's potential (pathos) create a compelling call to action. Her message is clear: Africa's future depends on removing barriers to entrepreneurship, and every individual has a role to play in making that vision a reality.

Overcoming Common Fears

Wade's presentation offers valuable lessons for overcoming three common fears: stating the obvious and being ignored, being criticized, and being forgotten.

Fear Of Stating The Obvious And Being Ignored

Lesson: This fear stems from the belief that addressing seemingly obvious issues will fail to resonate or make an impact because the audience may dismiss them as redundant or irrelevant. Wade confronts what might seem obvious: Systemic issues like bureaucracy and corruption stifle African entrepreneurship. Who among us hasn't been hindered by red tape in some way, even in something relatively small like getting a driver's license or a fishing permit?

Many people are aware of Africa's economic struggles, but Wade reframes this knowledge by exposing the underlying causes and linking them to real-world consequences. Her choice between violence and peaceful productivity confronts the audience with a moral crossroad: either continue tolerating the policies that cause despair, or remove the barriers to enterprise and unleash a future of dignity, prosperity, and peace.

Application

Transform Familiar Narratives Into Fresh Insights

- **Speak with clarity and precision:** Don't shy away from stating the obvious; instead, explain why it matters. For example, Wade contextualizes inefficiency as not just frustrating but life-destroying, as it perpetuates poverty.

- **Use concrete data to bolster the obvious:** When stating a point that seems widely understood, support it with numbers, examples, and real-life stories to show its depth. Wade's description of the World Bank's Doing Business report, which has fifty African countries at the bottom, turns a general truth into a concrete example and a call for reform.

- **Challenge misguided narratives:** Wade dismantles the "poverty-pity" mindset propagated by initiatives like Live Aid, Band Aid, and their current equivalents for unchecked foreign aid. She critiques the superficiality of these efforts, explaining that while well-meaning, they overlook the structural issues that perpetuate poverty and funnel resources into corrupt political hands. Her boldness reframes the obvious narrative—Africa's poverty—as a problem of systemic failure, not a lack of people trying to throw money at the problem.

Exercise

Gather a specific statistic that supports your argument and pair it with a personal or relatable story that demonstrates its impact. Practice presenting this combination aloud to make the obvious feel urgent and meaningful. Help your (imagined or real) audience see and feel why it matters.

Fear Of Being Criticized

Lesson: Speaking against popular narratives, especially those tied to humanitarian efforts, invites criticism. Wade's critique of the "We Are the World" mentality directly challenges deeply ingrained assumptions about aid and charity. Some people are shocked or angry at her rejection of foreign aid as the way to solve African poverty.

Wade exemplifies how to face criticism with confidence by grounding her arguments in evidence. Her critique of foreign aid is not merely an emotional rejection, but a reasoned argument: "We will stay stuck in an endless cycle of poverty until these chains are finally broken and our markets are set free." This logic disarms critics who might accuse her of lacking compassion.

---Application---

Stand Firm In The Face Of Criticism

- **Back your message with data:** Criticism is easier to withstand when you can point to undeniable facts. Wade critiques aid policies by highlighting how they fuel corruption instead of addressing root causes. Her logic makes her argument more difficult to dismiss as mere opinion.

- **Acknowledge opposing views while offering alternatives:** Wade acknowledges that the intention behind foreign aid programs to Africa is noble but misguided. By presenting entrepreneurship as the solution, she shifts the conversation from blame to action.

- **Use criticism to strengthen your argument:** Anticipate the backlash and address it head-on. Wade doesn't shy away from criticizing well-meaning aid movements, but she also offers a better path forward, making her message constructive rather than combative.

Exercise

Role-play a scenario where someone criticizes your ideas. Respond calmly, acknowledging the opposing view while pivoting to your core argument and offering a constructive alternative. For example, if criticized for opposing public schools, explain how tax breaks for homeschooling could solve lagging test scores or student disengagement.

Fear Of Being Forgotten

Lesson: Wade addresses this fear by tying her personal advocacy to a can-do spirit, providing a hopeful vision for Africa. Her statement, "So, I have this attitude in life: something is wrong, find a way to fix it. And that's why I started the business that I start," positions her voice within a grand, inspiring narrative. This vision makes her message memorable because it connects to a broader hope for Africa's future.

Application

Build A Legacy Through Visionary Messaging

- **Create a memorable vision:** Wade's dream of African entrepreneurs being celebrated globally is an image that sticks. To overcome the fear of being forgotten, focus on creating a vision that connects emotionally with your audience.

- **Embed your voice in the larger narrative:** Position yourself as part of an ongoing movement or story that matters to you. Wade is not just an entrepreneur; she's part of the larger fight for economic freedom in Africa. What are you fighting for?

- **Emphasize the stakes:** Wade's passion for Africa's future makes her message urgent and enduring. By explaining the can-do spirit, she draws a contrast to the present corruption and despair.

Exercise

Identify one human story that represents the stakes of your cause. Practice sharing this story in a way that conveys the real impact of your work, ensuring your message is both memorable and inspiring. Locate visual images that reflect the "before and after" of your message.

Wade's insights into Africa's entrepreneurial challenges, combined with her critique of the "poverty-pity" narrative, provide a unique lens for addressing specific fears about speaking out. These fears—fear of stating the obvious and being ignored, fear of being criticized, and fear of being forgotten—are common among those who aim to tackle entrenched narratives. Wade's approach offers practical lessons and applications for overcoming these fears.

Personal Connection: Blending Words And Actions

Magatte Wade is the only one of the "magnificent seven" speakers I've met in person, and it was an honor. She has a warm smile, a kind demeanor, and a fiery passion for her cause of building Africa into a prosperous continent. I'm all in on that goal. (Hopefully, this book can help toward that end.)

As you've seen, some material in this book emerged from a presentation I delivered in Nairobi in July 2024. I especially wanted to inspire local students (though there were students from dozens of countries) by featuring an African hero. Magatte Wade was the obvious choice.

In Nairobi, I met several African entrepreneurs I had previously coached via Zoom. It was a thrill to shake their hands in person. One whom I'd never met before was the Nigerian poet and speaker Ogochukwu Nancy Peter. After my presentation, Ogochukwu told me, "I appreciated Robert's use of slides and short videos to support his points, finding the practical examples and lessons from notable figures like Magatte Wade particularly engaging. He also mentioned incorporating elements from the presentation into his own work, indicating a deep learning experience and satisfaction with his participation in the event."[10] Ogochukwu's feedback underscores the transformative potential of effectively delivered speeches: By embracing and sharing powerful narratives like Wade's, individuals can spark significant change, promoting a new generation of leaders equipped to innovate and inspire in their communities and beyond.

Wade's work reminds me of the dynamic spirit of the cheetah—a metaphor she explores in her book *The Heart of a Cheetah*. While the elephant may be my favorite African animal (which I finally saw in person!), Wade uses the cheetah to symbolize the fast, agile entrepreneur who adapts and thrives. She contrasts the cheetah's entrepreneurial spirit with the slow-moving hippopotamus, representing bureaucracy and stagnation. She learned this analogy from her brilliant mentor, George Ayittey.[11]

Wade's message about the dignity of business ownership and perseverance reminds me of Kelly Senn, the entrepreneurial powerhouse behind Orlando Power Yoga. During one of her first classes as a new owner, a mouse darted across the studio. What would you do? Your business could be at stake if people found out. Kelly froze, panic rising—but no one else noticed. The tiny intruder scurried out the other door, never to be seen again. Crisis averted.

I saw an opportunity to coach Kelly on storytelling using this anecdote. I said, "Give the mouse some dialogue. Make him cocky. Give him an attitude. Make us feel like we were there. For instance, have the mouse stop, lock eyes with you, wink, and say, 'Yes, you thought Mickey was the only mouse who runs this town? Well, I do. And I'll be back. But for now, enjoy your class.'" Dialogue always makes stories more real and memorable.

Owning a business isn't just about running a company; it's about owning your narrative and staying composed under pressure. Kelly could have panicked and let the mouse ruin her class, just like an entrepreneur could let small setbacks derail their confidence. But instead, she stayed the course, just like she's done building Orlando Power Yoga into a thriving studio.

Perseverance in business, like in storytelling, means learning from every experience, even the unexpected ones. The best entrepreneurs, like the best speakers, don't just react to challenges; they shape them into something meaningful (or in this case, entertaining).

That's why Magatte Wade's message resonates. True dignity in business ownership comes from facing uncertainty with grit, adaptability, and sometimes a sense of humor.

Insights From Magatte Wade's Work

Wade's TEDGlobal talk and written works delve deeply into the barriers faced by African entrepreneurs and propose actionable solutions rooted in resilience, cultural shifts, and policy reforms. Below, I unpack three themes—navigating bureaucracy, cultural shifts, and economic freedom—with examples that bring her theories to life. Each is linked to lessons for liberty's leaders to support change.

Navigating Inefficient Bureaucracy

Wade vividly illustrates African entrepreneurs' challenges by recounting the bureaucratic problems of starting a business in Senegal. This acrobatic process of permits, inspections, and approvals drains potential entrepreneurs of time and resources. Wade recounts, "Did you know that for all my raw material that I can't find in the country, I have to pay a 45% tariff on everything that comes in?"[12] This highlights how red tape suffocates innovation and growth.

Wade calls for systemic reform to simplify business processes, emphasizing that Africa's youth cannot unleash their potential when they are buried under mountains of paperwork. By contrasting African countries' bureaucratic hurdles with the ease of starting a business in other countries, she underscores the dire need for change.

Lessons For Liberty's Leaders

- **Resilience and adaptability:** Leaders must persist despite structural barriers, advocating long-term reforms while navigating existing systems.

- **Simplification as a policy goal:** To encourage entrepreneurship, bureaucracy should be severely reduced. Leaders can push for deregulation and transparent processes to make starting and running a business less daunting.

Cultural Shifts: From Pity To Pride

Wade critiques the international narrative that paints Africa as a helpless continent needing charity: "Instead of building us up, they created a lasting image of Africa that trades on pity, not power." She calls this "poverty porn."[13] Instead, she highlights the need to promote pride in entrepreneurial achievement.

Through initiatives like sharing success stories of African entrepreneurs and creating mentorship opportunities, Wade demonstrates how changing the cultural mindset can empower individuals. She tells her own story as a Senegalese entrepreneur, holding this up as a beacon to inspire others to dream bigger.

Lessons For Liberty's Leaders

- **Inspire through example:** Leaders should share stories of local successes to build a culture that values self-reliance and innovation. Stories of humble beginnings leading to great things can inspire others to believe in themselves and take the first steps toward unleashing their potential.

- **Create support networks:** Establish programs to connect emerging entrepreneurs with mentors and resources that celebrate their achievements, rather than treating them as aid beneficiaries.

Economic Freedom And Personal Dignity

Wade emphasizes that real progress comes from reducing government interference and enhancing market forces. She discusses how empowering entrepreneurs and embracing free-market policies can spark economic growth and improve the lives of many. By referencing successful examples, such as Rwanda's economic transformation post genocide, Wade illustrates how promoting economic reforms and backing a business-friendly environment can significantly reduce poverty and stimulate prosperity across the continent.

Wade also acknowledges the profound dignity that comes when individuals are free to pursue work that aligns with their values. This freedom leads to personal satisfaction and development while also contributing to prosperity, as people are more motivated and productive when they engage in meaningful work.

Lessons For Liberty's Leaders

- **Promote free markets:** Leaders should champion policies that reduce government control and allow businesses to flourish independently, furthering competition and innovation.

- **Individual dignity through work:** Leaders should champion policies that emphasize the deep-seated value and satisfaction derived from freely pursuing work that resonates with one's values, enhancing both personal fulfillment and prosperity.

Wade's message extends beyond diagnosing problems to empowering individuals and leaders to act. Her lessons for liberty's leaders are clear:

- **Confront systemic challenges:** Like Wade, leaders must speak boldly about entrenched problems, even if their views challenge popular narratives.

- **Speak with clarity and conviction:** Wade's ability to connect personal stories with broader policy arguments makes her message compelling. Leaders should strive to communicate with both precision and passion.

- **Push for lasting change:** Wade's advocacy of deregulation and cultural shifts shows that transformative change requires persistence and a long-term vision.

By rejecting the "poverty-pity" narrative and championing the potential of African entrepreneurs, Wade teaches us that resilience, clarity, and vision are the keys to forwarding economic freedom and lasting progress. Her work is a call to action for liberty's leaders worldwide.

Wade's example challenges us not only to champion economic freedom but also to amplify the voices of those creating value through innovation and integrity. As liberty's leaders, our task now is to sustain the lessons we've learned and step boldly into the future, owning the stage with confidence, purpose, and the courage to inspire transformative change.

The final chapters focus on consolidating these gains, refining your delivery, and stepping forward into a future where your voice becomes an enduring force for liberty and progress. Now that we've analyzed the "magnificent seven" speakers, we'll transition to what to do next with these ideas and practices, particularly when things go wrong. Keep turning the pages if you want to know what it takes to gain and maintain the stage.

PART III

Owning
The Stage

CHAPTER 10

Minding Your Business When Things Go Wrong

Communication is two-sided—vital and profound communication
makes demands on those who are to receive it . . . .
[It] demands attentiveness, awareness, and the ability
to understand and interpret.

NIDO QUBEIN[1]

As you approach the end of this book, it's important to recognize that the task of becoming a voice of reason and liberty—a leader who inspires, influences, and transforms—is not a one-time effort. It's a continuous process of growth, adaptation, and refinement. The question you may now face is: "How do I take the tools, lessons, and breakthroughs I've gained and ensure they continue to serve me in the years to come, even when the path gets tough?"

Exploring Setbacks: Getting Started

The road ahead will be full of obstacles. Setbacks are inevitable, but they're also teachers. It's essential to embrace a mindset that views challenges as opportunities for refinement. Let's consider three common scenarios and explore how to troubleshoot them effectively.

Plateauing: When Progress Stalls

- **The challenge:** After experiencing significant improvement, you feel stuck. Your speeches, leadership, or business impact is no longer growing.

- **The solution:** Redefine success. Plateaus often signal a need to set higher goals or pursue a new challenge. Ask yourself:

  - "How can I push the boundaries of my comfort zone?"

  - "Is there a new skill I need to learn to reach the next level?"

  - "Can I mentor someone to reinforce and sharpen my expertise?"

- **Example in action:** A business leader who successfully motivates their team might decide to pursue keynote speaking opportunities to share their leadership philosophy on a larger scale. The new challenge reignites growth and builds credibility as a thought leader. For inspiration, you can think of how Martin Luther King, Jr.'s pivot from local activism to the national stage accelerated the Civil Rights movement.

Facing Criticism: When The Spotlight Brings Scrutiny

- **The challenge:** As you gain influence, critics will inevitably surface. Whether it's negative feedback on a speech or skepticism of your leadership, criticism can be a blow to confidence.

- **The solution:** Separate constructive criticism from noise. Use Aristotle's principles of rhetoric to assess whether feedback is valid. Ask:

  - "Does this criticism offer actionable insight (logos)?"

  - "Am I aligning my actions with my core principles (ethos)?"

  - "Am I addressing the right emotions (pathos) in my audience?"

- **Example in action:** Imagine delivering a keynote and receiving feedback that it felt "too theoretical." Rather than dismissing it, reflect on whether your logos (logic) overshadowed your pathos (emotional connection). Revise your next presentation to balance real-world examples with your intellectual framework. Ayn Rand herself faced criticism for the abstraction of her ideas. Still, rather than abandon her principles, she refined how she presented them, developing fictional stories and public lectures that helped clarify and humanize her philosophy.

Balancing Growth With Resilience: Avoiding Burnout

- **The challenge:** As your influence grows, so do demands on your time and energy. You may feel overwhelmed or begin to lose the passion that once fueled your work.

- **The solution:** Focus on intentional impact. Evaluate which opportunities align most with your values and goals and gracefully say no to the rest. Build habits that prioritize self-care and clarity:

  - Dedicate time weekly for reflection and recalibration.

  - Maintain a "nonnegotiable" boundary for personal recharge, such as family time or creative pursuits.

- **Example in action:** A rising entrepreneur might allocate specific days for strategic work and reserve evenings for personal development. This structure maintains momentum without diminishing mental and emotional health. Look how Frederick Douglass balanced speaking, writing, and running a business to ensure his voice remained powerful and profitable.

Leveling Up Your Troubleshooting With Ethos, Logos, And Pathos

Even the most polished speaker or leader will face setbacks. A misstep on stage, a failed business pitch, or an audience that simply doesn't respond as expected can leave you questioning your ability to lead. But setbacks aren't the end of the story. They're opportunities to refine your approach, grow stronger, and connect with your audience on a deeper level.

To take your troubleshooting skills to the next level, here is a five-step practical process for exploring and troubleshooting common setbacks, using Aristotle's ethos, logos, and pathos as your foundation.

Step 1: Diagnose The Setback

- **Ethos misstep:** Did your audience question your credibility or authority? For example, perhaps a statistic you cited was outdated, or your body language lacked confidence.

  - **Example:** Imagine pitching to investors with a monotone delivery and crossed arms. This is a stark contrast to Douglass's or Wade's commanding presence that inspired belief in their vision. Such misaligned body language erodes trust.

- **Logos misstep:** Was your argument unclear or unconvincing? Did you overload your audience with too much information for them to process, or fail to present evidence that supports your point?

  - **Example:** Perhaps you leaned too heavily on abstract ideas without grounding them in relatable examples. As Rand demonstrated in her West Point address, connecting philosophy to practical action with concrete examples meaningful to your audience is key.

- **Pathos misstep:** Did you fail to connect emotionally with your audience? Were you too detached, or did your emotional appeal not land with them?

  - **Example:** Martin Luther King, Jr.'s refrain, "I have a dream," moved millions because it connected deeply with their own hopes for the future. Without emotional resonance, even well-reasoned arguments can fall flat.

Step 2: Analyze The Cause
- **Ask reflective questions:**

  - **Ethos:** Was there a gap in your preparation or credibility? Did you fail to address audience skepticism up front?

  - **Logos:** Was your argument logical and clear? Did you provide enough evidence to make your point compelling?

  - **Pathos:** Did you tap into emotions that connect with your audience? Did your tone, stories, or examples evoke the right response?

- **Case study:** Let's say you gave a pitch at a networking event but didn't secure any follow-ups. Reflecting, you realize you introduced yourself with vague credentials like "I help people succeed," rather than specific examples of how your work creates measurable results. The audience may have questioned your ethos (credibility) because you didn't give them something concrete to trust. Empty promises are a dime a dozen. Tangible results are worth their weight in gold.

Step 3: Develop A Plan To Address The Setback
- **Ethos:** Rebuild trust

  - **Action plan:** Prepare anecdotes or case studies that highlight your credibility. For example, if your credibility was questioned during a sales pitch, follow up with a concise email showcasing a recent success story or testimonial.

- **Example:** Patrick Henry's impassioned cry, "Give me liberty, or give me death," resonated because his ethos was built on years of unwavering commitment to freedom.

Exercise

Develop a brief anecdote or case study that demonstrates your expertise or successful track record. Practice presenting this narrative confidently. You can set the scene, illustrate action, highlight results, and reflect on impact.

- **Logos:** Refine the argument
  - **Action plan:** Craft your message with clarity using the formula Problem ➡ Solution ➡ Result.

    - **Example:** After realizing your pitch lacked clarity, refine it with an engaging opener: "Did you know 80 percent of new entrepreneurs fail because they lack effective communication skills? That's why I developed a three-step coaching program that has helped over fifty clients achieve sustainable success."

Exercise

Build a structured argument following these steps: Select your argument. Define the problem. Present your solution. Illustrate the result. Practice. Get feedback. Then refine your argument to ensure your logic flows naturally.

Minding Your Business When Things Go Wrong | 151

- **Pathos:** Strengthen emotional connection

  - **Action plan:** Incorporate stories that humanize your message. Find anecdotes that illustrate your passion and commitment. Develop vivid imagery to move your audience to action.

    - **Example:** Churchill's "We Shall Fight on the Beaches" inspired hope by painting vivid images of resilience, a lesson in pathos that remains ageless.

Exercise

Stand in front of a mirror or record yourself telling an emotionally resonant story. Notice your tone and facial expressions. Does your passion shine through? If you think so, then try it again in front of a trusted friend and have them explain to you what it made them feel.

Step 4: Implement Feedback Loops

- **Gather feedback:**

  - **Ask a trusted peer or mentor to watch your presentations** or business pitches and identify areas for improvement. Frame it as: "What resonated? What could be stronger?"

  - **Example:** Make a presentation at BNI (Business Network International) and afterward ask the chapter members for specific feedback. "Did my value proposition come across clearly? Did my story resonate?"

- **Self-assess:**

  - **Record your presentations and watch them critically.** Evaluate your use of ethos, logos, and pathos. Were you balanced in integrating all three principles, or did one element dominate?

- **Tip:** Use a checklist: Did I establish trust? Was my argument logical? Did I evoke emotion?

Step 5: Create A Routine For Mastery
- **Sustain momentum:**
  - **Dedicate time weekly to practicing key skills**, such as storytelling, structuring arguments, and using open body language. Tie these to specific goals like improving your BNI pitches or refining a keynote speech.

Exercise
Practice delivering your "why I do what I do" story in sixty seconds to multiple audiences, tweaking based on feedback each time.

- **Expand your influence:**
  - **Create additional speaking opportunities.** For instance, present a short "spotlight" speech at a BNI meeting or sign up for a local Toastmasters event.
  - **Leverage opportunities to turn challenges into lessons.** If you overcame a misstep, share that story with others to inspire them. People love to learn how others bounced back from failure and overcame obstacles.

Illustrative Exercise
Troubleshoot And Refine A Key Message

1. Write your message:

- Original: "I help businesses grow."

- Revised with ethos, logos, pathos: "In the past year, I've helped three companies grow their revenue by 50 percent through strategic marketing plans. I remember one client who was on the verge of closing down. After working together, not only did they turn a profit, but they also hired two more employees. Let me show you how I can do the same for your business."

2. Deliver to a peer group:

- Present your refined message to a small group and gather feedback. Did it land? Was it clear, credible, and emotionally resonant?

3. Refine again:

- Incorporate feedback, adjust the tone, and test your revisions in a real-world setting.

Conclusion: Turning Setbacks Into Strengths

Setbacks are inevitable, but how you handle them builds your character and defines your growth. By diagnosing issues, applying the principles of ethos, logos, and pathos, and consistently refining your approach, you can turn challenges into opportunities. As a leader in any field, your ability to troubleshoot effectively ensures that your voice remains a powerful force for change, whether on stage, in business, or in your personal life.

One of the best presentations on dealing with setbacks comes from Dr. Willie Jolly in his TEDx talk, "Turning Setbacks into Comebacks."[2] He describes being fired from his job and being replaced by a karaoke machine. His positive attitude and ability to embrace change enabled him to continue living his American dream.

Instead of seeing a setback as the end of the road, you can consider it as the beginning of another quest. The tools you've acquired are not meant to be stored away; they are meant to be used, refined, and applied every day. As you mind your business, you'll discover that the true reward is not just financial success, but the fulfillment of your potential as a leader, a voice of reason, and a force for positive change in the world.

I often quote Hall of Fame speaker and business expert Ford Saeks: "It's not how much you know, but how well you execute." You'll find out more on how to execute excellently in the final chapter.

CHAPTER 11

How To Actualize
Your Potential

Success is not something that happens to you; it's something that happens because of you and because of the actions you take.

KEITH HARRELL[1]

We turn from exploring and analyzing the art of communication to focus on an arena where your voice and presence can translate into tangible results: the world of business and leadership. Excellence in Aristotle's rhetorical principles of ethos, logos, and pathos isn't only for public speeches. It can also be a cornerstone of success in building trusted relationships, driving innovation, and creating value. Whether you're presenting to an audience, leading a team, or forging connections in a professional network, your ability to inspire and persuade is your competitive edge.

Recently, I joined Business Network International (BNI),[2] where I've seen firsthand the profound importance of trust and collaboration in driving business success. BNI's emphasis on building meaningful connections, rooted in shared values and mutual benefit, reinforces a key lesson: in business as in life, the stage isn't owned by the loudest voice, but by the one who has integrity and purpose.

There is wisdom in these words attributed to Winston Churchill: "Courage is what it takes to stand up and speak; courage is also what it takes to sit down and listen." In this chapter, we'll explore how you can apply the principles of effective communication to both speaking and listening. Sharing the stage or leading it for a while creates opportunities for translating your experience and expertise into a legacy of freedom and prosperity.

This final chapter is not about repeating the successes you've already had; it's about evolving them into lasting impact. Whether you've already overcome fears, excelled in persuasion skills, or found your unique voice, this is where we explore how to maintain and develop that mastery and prepare for the unexpected, so that your potential turns into a sustained legacy of influence.

The "magnificent seven" leaders—from Patrick Henry's fearless rhetoric to Magatte Wade's entrepreneurial passion—demonstrate that greatness requires more than skill. It demands persistence, vision, and adaptability. Here's how to make that leap.

Actualizing Potential Through Application: Moving Beyond Theory

It's not enough simply to know the principles of ethos, logos, and pathos and to analyze others' presentations with this framework. The real power lies in their application across different aspects of your life. Let's look at how these principles can evolve from tools to long-term strategies.

Ethos: Building Legacy

- **Application:** Expand your credibility through action. Ethos grows over time as others witness your consistency, integrity, and expertise.
  - **Example:** A leader who consistently champions their team's success builds a reputation for acknowledging others' excellence.

This becomes a foundation for larger opportunities, such as invitations to join advisory boards or lead industry panels.

Reflection Exercise

Write down three ways you've built trust this year. Identify one area where you could strengthen your ethos by being more transparent or by leading through example. Also, think about how Lincoln's Gettysburg Address cemented his ethos, uniting a divided nation. Have you helped others navigate conflicts to a successful resolution?

Logos: Innovating With Logic

- **Application:** Use logic not just to persuade others, but to innovate and evolve. Logos can drive problem-solving, whether in business strategy, personal growth, or communication.

  - **Example:** A business owner identifies inefficiencies in their operations by analyzing data trends and implements a streamlined workflow that saves hours of work per week. The logical decision boosts morale and profitability. Look at how Magatte Wade connected deregulation to economic empowerment.

Reflection Exercise

Think of a recent challenge you faced. Break it down using a logos-driven framework:

- Define the problem clearly.
- Identify data or evidence related to the problem.
- Brainstorm alternative possible solutions.
- Identify which alternative is most feasible in your context.
- Create a logical plan of action that could achieve that outcome.

Pathos: Amplifying Emotional Connection

- **Application:** Deepen your ability to inspire by authentically connecting with others. Pathos grows when you move beyond surface-level engagement to truly understand your audience's pain points, needs, and emotions.

  - **Example:** An entrepreneur could benefit from adopting the approach of King's "I Have a Dream" speech. In a product pitch, rather than merely listing features, the entrepreneur can weave a narrative showing how the product can fulfill the audience's aspirations or solve a pressing problem, much like King illustrated a vision of equality and freedom that touched the hearts of his listeners. The method transforms the pitch into a story of possibility and change, creating an emotional bond with potential customers and making the product's impact feel personal and compelling.

Reflection Exercise

Before your next major communication effort, ask yourself:

- ○ "What do I want the audience to think, feel, or do after they hear my presentation?"

- ○ "Which personal story or real-world example will resonate most deeply?"

Sustaining The Legacy: Building For The Future

To truly actualize your potential, you must think about the long-term outcomes you want to achieve. This involves nurturing your growth and laying the groundwork for lasting impact.

Invest In Relationships

- **Why it matters:** Networks are lifelines for influence and opportunity. BNI has taught me firsthand the power of trust-based relationships in driving success. I also am a big believer in having an accountability buddy. I have several for different aspects of my life, but none are more reliable, more enjoyable, and hold me as accountable as my best friend and musical partner, Michael Gresh. (I could write an entire book about what I've gained from him over the decades, but for now I'll leave my expression of deep gratitude at that.)

- **Action step:** Identify five key relationships in your personal and professional life. How can you deepen those connections? Whether it's a thoughtful thank-you note, an invitation to collaborate, or simply showing up when it matters, invest in those who uplift your journey.

Embrace Lifelong Learning

- **Why it matters:** The world is ever-changing, and staying relevant means staying curious.

- **Action step:** Commit to a "learn-and-apply" mindset. Identify one way to implement each new skill or insight you gain immediately. For example, you could do the following:
  - Attend a public speaking workshop, then volunteer to speak at a community event.
  - Read a book on leadership, then apply one principle in your next team meeting.

Define Your Version Of Success

- **Why it matters:** Success is deeply personal, so clarity on your goals ensures that you stay true to yourself and your purpose. This is a matter of integrity, motivation, and pride.

- **Action step:** Reflect on your legacy. What do you want people to most remember you for five years from now? Write down one sentence that captures your vision for the future. Use it as a guiding light when making decisions.

The Journey Continues: Speaking With Purpose LLC

Remember that this book is just the beginning as you continue to apply the lessons you've learned. Whether you're refining your public speaking skills, developing your leadership capabilities, or seeking to make a lasting impact through your work, the journey of growth and improvement is the journey of a lifetime.

That's where Speaking With Purpose LLC comes in. My business is dedicated to helping individuals like you continue their goal of becoming effective, impactful communicators and leaders. Through our courses, one-on-one coaching, and a wealth of resources available on our website www.speakingwithpurpose.llc, you'll find ongoing support to sustain and enhance your progress.

Courses

Our structured courses are designed to introduce you to and then deepen your understanding of communication strategies and leadership principles. Whether you're just starting out or looking to refine your skills, there's a course tailored to your needs.

One-On-One Coaching

Personalized coaching sessions offer you the opportunity to work directly with me. Together, we can address specific challenges, set goals, and develop a customized plan for your continued growth. Coaching is a powerful way to stay accountable and ensure that you're consistently moving forward.

Resources

Our website is a treasure trove of articles, videos, and tools that you can use to stay informed and inspired. Whether you're preparing for a major presentation or simply looking for a boost in motivation, you'll find what you need to stay on track.

Summary And Farewell

You've reached the end of this book, but the lessons and strategies you've learned are meant to be applied throughout your life. Remember, the principles of ethos, logos, and pathos are not just tools for public speaking. They're tools for effective communication in all aspects of life. Whether you're leading a team, building a business, or engaging with people in your community, these principles will serve you well.

Thank you for allowing me to be a part of your journey. Remember that Speaking With Purpose LLC is here to support you whenever you need guidance, inspiration, or just a bit of encouragement. The journey to becoming a voice of reason and liberty is never complete, but every step is meaningful. Whether inspired by Douglass's resilience, Rand's logic, or King's dream, your path is uniquely yours.

Here's to your continued growth and impact. May your future be filled with purpose, passion, and prosperity!

Acknowledgments

I am deeply grateful to my dear parents, Peter and Theresa Begley, for raising me with unwavering love, discipline, and a deep sense of purpose. Their strength, devotion, and values continue to guide me every day. The warmth, wisdom, and steady encouragement of my beloved oldest sister, Theresa, lives on in everything I do. This book is, in part, a tribute to their memory.

My gratitude to my dearest, Carrie-Ann Biondi, is both personal and professional. She sharpens my mind and fills my heart. Her love, wisdom, and philosophical clarity have enriched every part of this project with her thoughtful editing, detailed proofreading, and unending encouragement.

My cherished siblings, Evelyn, Marian, Damian (who proofread the entire book draft), David, Petra, Daria, and Peter, have shaped my journey in unique ways. I also thank my extended family, including my courageous cousins Anthony (NYPD) and Nicky (FDNY) Liso.

Those who generously read and commented on early drafts deserve special thanks for offering thoughtful insights that helped sharpen the message and deepen the book's impact: Daniel Modell, Joseph Kellard, Joel Schottenfeld, Steve Cohen, Antonio Valles, Buffi Gresh, and especially

Michael Gresh (my best friend for decades who knows how to deliver tough feedback with a gentle touch).

Richard Salsman and Andrew Bernstein have been beacons of reason and resilience for over forty years. Special thanks to James S. Valliant, Felipe Diego Gomides, and Leopold Ajami for their guidance, feedback, and contributions that elevated this book.

My speaking coaches and mentors—Darren LaCroix, Mark Brown, Ford Saeks, Chris McGuire, Michael Davis, Jennifer Leone, Ed Tate, and, of course, Craig Valentine—have all amazed and inspired me with their generosity and mastery of the craft. I strive every day—and through every page of this book—to pass their wisdom forward.

Kelly Senn and her dedicated staff at Orlando Power Yoga created a space of strength and focus where I was able to think through the ideas for this book. Xavier Hart's fabulous video editing of my group coaching calls elevated the quality and impact of our sessions, helping me connect more with my speaking coachees. Mark Da Cunha captured me at my best through his photography.

I appreciate Marsha Familaro Enright and Duncan Scott for graciously allowing me to step away from work obligations in order to focus on completing this book.

The Florida State University College Libertarians were early supporters of the ideas expressed here by offering me occasions to speak, for which I thank them.

I also owe thanks to Jeffrey Baldwin and Levi Baldwin as well as the LIBRE Institute for their practical framework and inspiring mission of supporting Latinos in the United States to lift their voices and live their dreams.

A special tribute goes to two heroic immigrants, Fengsuo Zhang and Jose Mora, whose incredible bravery in escaping tyranny to pursue the American dream has moved and inspired me beyond words. Their stories are living proof of what courage and freedom can achieve. This book reflects how much their voices and experiences—and those of many more I might be forgetting—have influenced my life and ideas.

About The Author

Born and raised in New York City in a large, loving family, Robert Begley built his career on consistency and purpose. He achieved over a decade of perfect attendance at Merrill Lynch, reflecting a lifelong commitment to showing up and delivering excellence. In 2004, he founded the New York Heroes Society to celebrate champions of liberty. In 2023, he launched Speaking With Purpose LLC to help business leaders and entrepreneurs speak with courage, clarity, and confidence.

A seasoned speaker and certified World Class Speaking Coach, Robert has addressed audiences internationally and across the United States, including appearances on national television. His clients include entrepreneurs, C-level executives, police captains, and immigrants who have escaped tyranny, some of whom were inspired by Robert's mission to unleash their voices to make a difference.

Outside of speaking, Robert pursues physical vitality and personal growth. He has completed seven New York City Marathons, danced ballet on stage, practices Bikram yoga, swims, cycles, and strength trains regularly. A world traveler, he has explored all fifty US states and six continents. He donates blood six times a year and belongs to high-impact communities including Business Network International, Toastmasters International,

Stage Time University, Brian Johnson's Heroic, Donald Miller's Business Made Simple, Benjamin Hardy's Rapid Transformation program, and the Radical Agreement Project improv group.

Robert is also a lover of culture—music, theater, and visual arts—and fuels his mind by reading and listening to more than one hundred books annually. He now lives in Orlando, Florida, with his dearest, Carrie-Ann Biondi.

Works Cited
And Author's Notes

Chapter 1   The Joy Of Speaking And Why It Matters

1   Les Brown, "7 Principles of Powerful Storytelling," n.d., https://lesbrown.com/7-principles/book, p. 3.

2   Chip Heath and Dan Heath, *Made to Stick: Why Some Ideas Survive and Others Die* (Random House, 2007), p. 278.

3   John Medina, *Brain Rules: 12 Principles for Surviving and Thriving at Work, Home, and School*, 2nd ed. (Pear Press, 2014), p. 72.

4   John Stuart Mill, *On Liberty* (1859; repr., Penguin Classics, 1985), p. 76.

5   Eric Patterson, "Glossophobia (Fear of Public Speaking): Signs, Symptoms, & Treatments," medical review by Naveed Saleh, *Choosing Therapy*, March 9, 2023, https://www.choosingtherapy.com/glossophobia/. This data comes from this article by Alexandre Heeren, Grazia Ceschi, David P. Valentiner, Vincent Dethier, and Pierre Philippot, "Assessing Public Speaking Fear with the Short Form of the Personal Report of Confidence as a Speaker Scale: Confirmatory Factor Analyses Among a French-Speaking Community Sample," *Neuropsychiatric Disease and Treatment* 9 (May 2013): 609–618, https://doi.org/10.2147/NDT.S43097, in their note 1 for their claim (which they put at 77 percent). Heeren et al. got their report from this report by Tomas Furmark, Maria Tillfors, P.-O. Evers, Ina Marteinsdottir, Ola Gefvert, and Mats Fredrikson, "Social Phobia in the General Population: Prevalence and Sociodemographic Profile," *Social Psychiatry*

and Psychiatric Epidemiology 34, no. 8 (1999): 416–24, https://doi. org/10.1007/s001270050163. This report claims that 145 people out of 288 reported having "social phobia," 77 percent of those 145 people reported being afraid of public speaking. That makes about 24 percent of the 288 people afraid of public speaking. This is a relatively small population surveyed in different countries.

6   "Studies Confirm the Power of Visuals to Engage Your Audience in eLearning," Sh!ft (blog), accessed April 25, 2025, https://www. shiftelearning.com/blog/bid/350326/studies-confirm-the-power-of-visuals-in-elearning.

7   Michael Schneider, "Costs of Poor Communication Reach $37 Billion. Avoid Disconnects By Implementing These Two Things," Inc.com, July 11, 2018, https://www.inc.com/michael-schneider/the-extrovert-vs-introvert-dynamic-could-be-costing-your-organization-millions-heres-how-to-bridge-communication-gap.html.

8   Katherine Brodsky, *No Apologies: How to Find and Free Your Voice in the Age of Outrage* (Pitchstone Publishing, 2024), p. 17.

Chapter 2   The Blueprint For Finding Your Voice

1   Aristotle, *Rhetoric*, in Plato and Aristotle, *Gorgias and Rhetoric*, trans. and ed. Joe Sachs (Focus Publishing, 2009), p. 137.

2   Patricia Fripp, Darren LaCroix, and Mark Brown, *Deliver Unforgettable Presentations: How to Speak to Be Remembered and Repeated In-Person, Online, and Onstage* (Indie Books International, 2022), p. 19.

3   Aristotle, *Rhetoric*, ed. Sachs, p. 137.

4   Aristotle, *Rhetoric*, ed. Sachs, p. 138.

5   Aristotle, *Rhetoric*, ed. Sachs, p. 138.

6   Aristotle, *Rhetoric*, ed. Sachs, p. 138.

7   Aristotle, *Rhetoric*, ed. Sachs, p. 173.

8   Aristotle, *Rhetoric*, ed. Sachs, p. 138.

9   Aristotle, *Rhetoric*, ed. Sachs, p. 140.

10 Aristotle, *Rhetoric*, ed. Sachs, p. 138.

11 Aristotle, *Rhetoric*, ed. Sachs, p. 194.

12 Walter Sylesh, correspondence to author, August 23, 2024.

Chapter 3   An Enlightenment Voice Of Reason

1   Thomas Paine, "The American Crisis," December 1776, https://www.loc. gov/resource/cph.3b06889/, p. 1.

2   "Patrick Henry Delivering His Celebrated Speech," *Encyclopedia Virginia*, accessed April 6, 2025, https://encyclopediavirginia. org/1658hpr-9260362296ba000/.

3   Patrick Henry, "Give Me Liberty or Give Me Death," in *The World's Great Speeches: 292 Speeches from Pericles to Mandela*, 4th ed., ed. Lewis Copeland, Lawrence W. Lamm, and Stephen J. McKenna (Dover Publications, Inc., 1999), pp. 232–34. All subsequent quotations from this speech are from these pages.

4   Henry, in *World's Great*, p. 232.

5   Henry, in *World's Great*, p. 232.

6   Henry, in *World's Great*, p. 232.

7   Henry, in *World's Great*, p. 232.

8   Henry, in *World's Great*, pp. 232-33.

9   Henry, in *World's Great*, p. 232.

10   Henry, in *World's Great*, p. 233.

11   Henry, in *World's Great*, p. 233.

12   Henry Mayer, *A Son of Thunder: Patrick Henry and the American Republic* (Grove Press, 1991), p. 280.

13   Henry, in *World's Great*, p. 233.

14   Mayer, *Son of Thunder*, pp. 281–82.

15   Jon Kukla, *Patrick Henry: Champion of Liberty* (Simon & Schuster, 2017), p. 302.

16   Ron Chernow, *Alexander Hamilton* (Penguin Books, 2005), p. 76.

17   Fengsuo Zhang, in correspondence with Robert Begley, July, 2024.

18   "Tiananmen Square: Rarely Seen Video of the 1989 Protests in China," *CNN Rewind*, written by Allison Brown, directed by Samantha Stamler, aired December 5, 2022, on CNN, posted December 5, 2022, YouTube,

17 min., 35 sec., https://www.youtube.com/watch?v=uuoXCki1jss&ab_channel=CNN10.

19 "A Conversation with Koala, a Survivor of the 2015 '709 Crackdown,'" *HRIC Weekly Brief,* Human Rights in China, July 9, 2024, https://hrichina.substack.com/p/a-conversation-with-koala-a-survivor.

Chapter 4   Conceived In Liberty

1   "Remarks in Response to a Serenade," American Presidency Project, accessed April 7, 2025, https://www.presidency.ucsb.edu/documents/remarks-response-serenade-3.

2   Stephen Moore and Julian L. Simon, *It's Getting Better All the Time: 100 Greatest Trends of the Last 100 Years* (Cato Institute, 2000), pp. 254–55.

3   Christopher Klein, "Why the Gettysburg Address Is One of the Most Famous Speeches in History," History.com, last updated January 31, 2025, https://www.history.com/news/gettysburg-address-lincoln-speech-impact.

4   Abraham Lincoln, "The Gettysburg Address," in *The World's Great Speeches*, 4th ed., ed. Lewis Copeland, Lawrence W. Lamm, and Stephen J. McKenna (Dover Publications, Inc., 1999), pp. 314–15.

5   Paine, "American Crisis," p. 1.

6   "Abraham Lincoln as a Speaker," William H. Herndon letter, July 19, 1887, and Abram Bergen, in *Intimate Memories of Lincoln*, as quoted in Abraham Lincoln Online, accessed April 7, 2025, https://www.abrahamlincolnonline.org/lincoln/speeches/speaker.htm.

7   "Lincoln's Way with Words," Abraham Lincoln Online, accessed April 7, 2025, http://144.208.79.222/~abraha21/alo/lincoln/mind/index.htm.

8   *Frederick Douglass—Ultimate Collection: Complete Autobiographies, Speeches & Letters* (Musaicum Books, OK Publishing, Kindle Edition, 2018), location 18604.

9   "Evidence for the Unpopular Mr. Lincoln," American Battlefield Trust, accessed April 7, 2025, https://www.battlefields.org/learn/articles/evidence-unpopular-mr-lincoln.

10 Abraham Lincoln, *Speeches and Letters of Abraham Lincoln, 1832-1865. Abraham Lincoln: 16th President of the United States from 1861 to His Assassination in 1865* (Prabhat Prakashan, 2020), p. 213.

11 Edward Everett, "Gettysburg Address," accessed April 8, 2025, https:// voicesofdemocracy.umd.edu/everett-gettysburg-address-speech-text/.

Chapter 5   Becoming Self-Made

1   Frederick Douglass, "A Plea for Free Speech in Boston," December 9, 1860, accessed April 8, 2025, Foundation for Individual Rights and Expression, https://www.thefire.org/research-learn/plea-freedom-speech-boston.

2   Frederick Douglass, *Narrative of the Life of Frederick Douglass, An American Slave* (New American Library, 1968), p. vii.

3   Douglass, *Narrative*, p. 49.

4   Douglass, *Narrative*, p. 104.

5   Frederick Douglass, *Frederick Douglass—Ultimate Collection, Complete Autobiographies: Speeches and Letters, My Escape from Slavery, Narrative of the Life of Frederick Douglass, My Bondage and My Freedom* (DigiCat, 2023), 17,490.

6   Douglass, *Frederick Douglass—Ultimate Collection*, 17,325.

7   Douglass, *Frederick Douglass—Ultimate Collection*, 17,372.

8   Douglass, *Frederick Douglass—Ultimate Collection*, 17,389.

9   Douglass, *Frederick Douglass—Ultimate Collection*, 17,343.

10 Douglass, *Frederick Douglass—Ultimate Collection*, 17,347.

11 Douglass, *Frederick Douglass—Ultimate Collection*, 17,478.

12 Douglass, *Frederick Douglass—Ultimate Collection*, 17,510.

13 Douglass, *Frederick Douglass—Ultimate Collection*, 17,501.

14 Douglass, *Frederick Douglass—Ultimate Collection*, 17,506.
    In his *Politics*, Aristotle states, "Why a human being is an animal meant for a city, more than every sort of bee and every sort of herd animal, is clear. For nature, as we claim, does nothing uselessly, and a human being, alone among the animals, has speech." Speech here means logos or

reason. See Aristotle, *Politics*, trans. and ed. Joe Sachs (Focus Publishing, 2012), p. 3.

15 Douglass, *Frederick Douglass—Ultimate Collection,* 17,347.

16 Douglass, *Frederick Douglass—Ultimate Collection,* 17,509.

17 Douglass, *Frederick Douglass—Ultimate Collection,* 17,340.

18 Douglass, *Frederick Douglass—Ultimate Collection,* 17,357.

19 Douglass, *Frederick Douglass—Ultimate Collection,* 17,388.

20 Amos Paul Kennedy, Jr., *Once You Learn to Read, You Will Be Forever Free*, 2010, color letterpress print, 20 x 15 cm, Library of Congress, control number 2023634976, https://www.loc.gov/item/2023634976/.

Chapter 6   Contrasting Tyrants With A Leader

1 Winston Churchill, "The Scaffolding of Rhetoric," November 1897, accessed April 8, 2025, https://winstonchurchill.org/wp-content/uploads/2016/06/THE_SCAFFOLDING_OF_RHETORIC.pdf.

2 Stan Lee, "Spider-Man!," *Amazing Fantasy #15 Comic Book*, Illustrator: Steve Ditko (Marvel Comics, August 1962), https://quoteinvestigator.com/2015/07/23/great-power/#28524953-e2df-4927-92dc-ad18c36647e9.

3   Vladimir Lenin, *The State and Revolution*, Chapter 1, accessed April 8, 2025, https://www.marxists.org/archive/lenin/works/1917/staterev/ch01.htm#s4.

4 Adolf Hitler, *Mein Kampf,* trans. James Murphy, vol. 1, ch. X, Project Gutenberg of Australia, September 2002, https://gutenberg.net.au/ebooks02/0200601.txt.

5 Martin Gilbert, *Winston Churchill: The Wilderness Years* (Houghton Mifflin Harcourt, 1982).

6 Winston S. Churchill, *Never Give In! The Best of Winston Churchill's Speeches* (Hyperion, 2003), pp. 210–18, 245.

7 Churchill, *Never Give In*, p. 218.

8 Churchill, *Never Give In*, p. 214.

9 Churchill, *Never Give In*, p. 211.

10 Churchill, *Never Give In*, p. 212.

11 Churchill, *Never Give In*, p. 229.

12 Churchill, *Never Give In*, p. 218.

13 Churchill, *Never Give In*, p. 218.

14 Churchill, *Never Give In*, p. 218.

15 Churchill, *Never Give In*, p. 218.

16 James C. Humes, *Speak Like Churchill, Stand Like Lincoln: 21 Powerful Secrets of History's Greatest Speakers* (Three Rivers Press, 2002), p. xii.

17 "Winston Churchill Denies He Was a Warmonger Who Helped Bring on World War I," RAAB Collection, accessed April 8, 2025, https://www.raabcollection.com/winston-churchill-autograph/winston-churchill-signed-winston-churchill-denies-he-was-warmonger-who.

18 Churchill, *Never Give In*, p. 229.

19 Churchill, *Never Give In*, p. 245.

20 *The King's Speech*, directed by Tom Hooper (Momentum Pictures, 2010).

21 Churchill, *Never Give In*, p. 245.

Chapter 7   Content Of Character Versus Color Of Skin

1   Martin Luther King, Jr., *I Have a Dream: Writings and Speeches that Changed the World*, ed. James M. Washington (HarperCollins Publishing, 1992), p. 197.

2   Robert Begley, "Jackie Robinson: The Best Kind of American Hero," April 14, 2018, https://theobjectivestandard.com/2018/04/jackie-robinson-the-best-kind-of-american-hero/.

3   King, Jr., *I Have a Dream*, pp. 101–6.

4   King, Jr., *I Have a Dream*, p. 102.

5   King, Jr., *I Have a Dream*, p. 103.

6   King, Jr., *I Have a Dream*, p. 103.

7   King, Jr., *I Have a Dream*, p. 104.

8   King, Jr., *I Have a Dream*, p. 105.

9   James Truslow Adams, *The Epic of America* (Little, Brown, and Company, 1931), p. 404.

10 King, Jr., *I Have a Dream*, p. 98.

11 Bev-Freda Jackson, "Gospel Singer Mahalia Jackson Made a Suggestion During the 1963 March on Washington—and It Changed a Good Speech to a Majestic Sermon on an American Dream," The Conversation, accessed April 6, 2025, https://theconversation.com/gospel-singer-mahalia-jackson-made-a-suggestion-during-the-1963-march-on-washington-and-it-changed-a-good-speech-to-a-majestic-sermon-on-an-american-dream-212067.

12 Video testimonial from Sumaira Waseem for Robert Begley, July 26, 2024, https://www.youtube.com/shorts/hsha-6wETfo.

13 King, Jr., I Have a Dream, p. 104.

14 King, Jr., I Have a Dream, p. 105.

15 Martin Luther King, Jr., "Martin Luther King, Jr's 'I Have a Dream Full Speech Restored,'" speech at the March on Washington for Jobs and Freedom, August 28, 1963, posted January 7, 2023, by Notelu, YouTube, 17 min., 17 sec., https://www.youtube.com/watch?v=8LWuu2Zwsfs.

16 Ayn Rand, The Virtue of Selfishness (Signet, 1964), p. 176.

17 Nathaniel Branden, Who Is Ayn Rand? An Analysis of Ayn Rand's Works, with a biographical study by Barbara Branden (Paperback Library, 1964), p. 186.

Chapter 8   A Philosophy For Living On Earth

1 Ayn Rand, Philosophy: Who Needs It (New American Library, 1984), p. 276.

2 Rand, The Virtue of Selfishness, p. 14.

3 Branden, Who Is Ayn Rand?, p. 159.

4 David Henderson, "Johnny Carson Interviews Ayn Rand," EconLog (blog), Econlib, June 9, 2022, https://www.econlib.org/johnny-carson-interviews-ayn-rand/.

5 Shoshana Milgram, "Behind the Scenes: Ayn Rand's West Point Lecture (1974–2024)," presentation at OCON in Anaheim, CA, June 14, 2024, posted September 30, 2024, by Ayn Rand Institute, YouTube, 1 hr., 26 min., 22 sec., https://www.youtube.com/watch?v=V8yIcXmoAnQ&ab_channel=AynRandInstitute.

6 Rand, *Philosophy*, pp. 1–14.

7 Rand, *Philosophy*, pp. 2–3.

8 Rand, *Philosophy*, pp. 14–15.

9 Rand, *Philosophy*, p. 7.

10 Rand, *Philosophy*, p. 13.

11 Rand, *Philosophy*, p. 4.

12 Rand, *Philosophy*, pp. 4–5.

13 Rand, *Philosophy*, pp. 10–11.

14 Rand, *Philosophy*, p. 11.

15 Rand, *Philosophy*, p. 13.

16 Rand, *Philosophy*, p. 13.

17 Robert Begley and Carrie-Ann Biondi, "Robert Begley: PBS Great American Read—Ayn Rand," discussing *Atlas Shrugged*, October 18, 2018, posted October 24, 2018, by Robert Begley, YouTube, 2 min., 46 sec., https://www.youtube.com/watch?v=TK4LYRR9OD0&ab_channel=RobertBegley.

18 Robert Begley, "Robert Begley: The Voice of Reason. Richard Salsman on Gold and Liberty," interview with Richard M. Salsman, October 1996, posted May 20, 2017, by Robert Begley, YouTube, 56 min., 27 sec., https://www.youtube.com/watch?v=szGWvAvvZUw&ab_channel=RobertBegley.

19 Jack NiCastro, video testimonial for Robert Begley, April 21, 2024, https://www.youtube.com/shorts/zwCLPVaID3s.

20 Amanda de Vasconcellos, "Amanda Testimonial," video testimonial for Robert Begley, July 26, 2024, posted February 20, 2025, by Robert Begley, Vimeo, 1 min., 12 sec., https://vimeo.com/1058778291.

21 Dan Modell, correspondence to author, October–December 2024.

22 Modell, correspondence to author.

23 Modell, correspondence to author.

24 Modell, correspondence to author.

25 Edgard Mugenzi, video testimonial for Robert Begley, July 26, 2024, https://www.youtube.com/shorts/CaTWhDXk5Jw.

Chapter 9   From Poverty To Prosperity

1   Magatte Wade, *The Heart of A Cheetah: How We Have Been Lied to about African Poverty—and What That Means for Human Flourishing* (Cheetah Press, 2023), p. 30.

2   Magatte Wade, "Why It's Too Hard to Start a Business in Africa—and How to Change It," TEDGlobal, Arusha, Tanzania, August 2017, 9 min., 2 sec., https://www.ted.com/talks/magatte_wade_why_it_s_too_hard_to_start_a_business_in_africa_and_how_to_change_it?

3   Wade, "Why It's Too Hard to Start a Business in Africa—and How to Change It," TEDGlobal, August 2017, 2 min., 10 sec.

4   Wade, "Why It's Too Hard to Start a Business in Africa—and How to Change It," TEDGlobal, August 2017, 5 min., 13 sec.

5   Wade, "Why It's Too Hard to Start a Business in Africa—and How to Change It," TEDGlobal, August 2017, 5 min., 10 sec.

6   Wade, "Why It's Too Hard to Start a Business in Africa—and How to Change It," TEDGlobal, August 2017, 3 min., 30 sec.

7   Wade, "Why It's Too Hard to Start a Business in Africa—and How to Change It," TEDGlobal, August 2017, 8 min., 1 sec.

8   Wade, *The Heart of A Cheetah*, p. 10.

9   Wade, "Why It's Too Hard to Start a Business in Africa—and How to Change It," TEDGlobal, August 2017, 8 min., 15 sec.

10   Ogochukwu Nancy Peter, "Ogochukwu Testimonial," testimonial for Robert Begley, July 26, 2024, posted February 20, 2025, by Robert Begley, Vimeo, 53 sec., https://vimeo.com/1058779273.

11   George Ayittey, "African Cheetahs Versus Hippos," TEDGlobal, Arusha, Tanzania, June 2007, 17 min., 35 sec., https://www.ted.com/talks/george_ayittey_africa_s_cheetahs_versus_hippos?subtitle=en.

12   Wade, "Why It's Too Hard to Start a Business in Africa—and How to Change It," TEDGlobal, August 2017, 4 min., 38 sec.

13   Magatte Wade, "Stop Pitying Africans: Why Pity Keeps Our People Poor," *Africa's Bright Future* (blog), July 6, 2023, https://magatte.substack.com/p/stop-pitying-africans-why-pity-keeps.

Chapter 10   Minding Your Business When Things Go Wrong

1   Nido R. Qubein, *How to Be a Great Communicator: In Person, on Paper, and on the Podium* (John Wiley & Sons, 1996), p. 23.

2   Dr. Willie Jolley, "Turning Setbacks into Comebacks," TEDxNASA, posted November 22, 2010, by TEDx Talks, YouTube, 13 min., 50 sec., https://www.youtube.com/watch?v=df8xrf23Ung&ab_channel=TEDxTalks.

Chapter 11   How To Actualize Your Potential

1   Keith Harrell, *Attitude Is Everything: 10 Life-Changing Steps to Turning Attitude into Action* (HarperCollins, 2005), p. 15.

2   For Business Network International, see: https://www.bni.com/. My particular club is New York City's Chapter 64: https://manhattanbni.com/en-US/chapterdetail?chapterId=8qcf6pJ0Y1eoQMpkW8CkkA%3D%3D&name=BNI+Manhattan+64.

Index